D1270806

Color Forecasting

ACCESSOIRES DE LA TABLE   MODERN GRAPHIC

ACCESSOIRES DE LA TABLE   AVANT-GARDE COULEUR

ACCESSOIRES DE LA TABLE   MODERNE CHROMATIC

ACCESSOIRES DE LA TABLE   BAROQUE CHROMATIC

ACCESSOIRES DE LA TABLE   SYMPHONIE DECORATIVE

ACCESSOIRES DE LA TABLE   COMPAGNIE DES INDES

ACCESSOIRES DE LA TABLE   CEREMONIAL PRECIEUX

ACCESSOIRES DE LA TABLE   ETHNIQUE NATUREL

Color Forecasting
A Survey of International Color Marketing

Harold Linton

VNR VAN NOSTRAND REINHOLD
_____New York

Copyright © 1994 by Harold Linton

Library of Congress Catalog Card Number 93-26500
ISBN 0-442-01160-1

I(T)P Van Nostrand Reinhold is an International Thomson Publishing company.
ITP logo is a trademark under license.

Printed in Singapore

Van Nostrand Reinhold
115 Fifth Avenue
New York, NY 10013

International Thomson Publishing GmbH
Königswinterer Straße 418
53227 Bonn
Germany

International Thomson Publishing
Berkshire House, 168-173
High Holborn, London WC1V 7AA
England

International Thomson Publishing Asia
221 Henderson Building #05-10
Singapore 0315

Thomas Nelson Australia
102 Dodds Street
South Melbourne 3205
Victoria, Australia

International Thomson Publishing Japan
Kyowa Building, 3F
2-2-1 Hirakawacho
Chiyoda-ku, Tokyo 102
Japan

Nelson Canada
1120 Birchmount Road
Scarborough, Ontario
M1K 5G4, Canada

KHL 16 15 14 13 12 11 10 9 8 7 6 5 4 3 2 1

Library of Congress Cataloging in Publication Data

Linton, Harold.
      Color forecasting : a survey of international color marketing /
Harold Linton.
           p.   cm.
      Includes bibliographical references and index.
      ISBN 0-442-01160-1
      1. Color—United States—Specimen.   2. Color—United States—
Marketing.   3. Color in industry.   I. Title.
QC495.2.L56   1994
381'.45667'0973—dc20   93-26500
                                                  CIP

To Deeni, Ruth, and Millie

FULL-PAGE IMAGES

Frontispiece—*Trends of colors and dominant decor expressed in 1991 in decorative tableware.* This industry is closely linked to household linens and decoration accessories. The eight dominant trends: Modern Graphic, Modern Chromatic, Decorative Symphony, Precious Ceremonial, Avant-garde color, Baroque Chromatic, India Company, Natural Ethnic. The designation of segments voluntarily appeals to evocative words destined to illustrate each segment in a manner of imagery. Courtesy of Atelier 3D Couleur/Jean-Philippe Lenclos.

Page 10—Trends of colors and dominant decor in household linens in 1991. Courtesy of Atelier 3D Couleur/Jean-Philippe Lenclos (see also figure caption 49).

Page 60—*G.I. Joe* (Hasbro Showrooms, U.S.A.): Although G.I. Joe is essentially a military concept, it has become over the years more of a part of our youth culture (without passing judgement as to being good or bad). The space was designed to reflect several important points: 1) Confidence and presence in the marketplace based on the historic success of the product. 2) Innovation of product and willingness to experiment—not taking their leadership position for granted. 3) Reinforcement of the cartoon aspect of play—as a reminder of how the play pattern works and a way of distancing the product from the reality of the military.

Page 94—Printed duvet and pillowcase set with plain dye reversible quilt in Dormas 1992 Home Furnishings Collection, with matching reversible pillowcases with studs as a new product development to give a totally reversible look.

Page 146—Bibb Hospitality, Candlelight Tablelinen. Courtesy of Bibb Company and Leatrice Eiseman.

Page 168—*Native American Color.* Courtesy of Merle Linby-Young.

Page 188—"Fresco" presentation board used to demonstrate use of mid-tone tinted jewels. Courtesy of Diane Clavert.

Page 210—Cachet makes it surprisingly easy to turn an original scan into an image suitable for publication, (lower righthand image). Cachet's MultiChoice option makes it easy to correct an image by choosing the alternative you like best (images top and bottom center).

Contents

Foreword

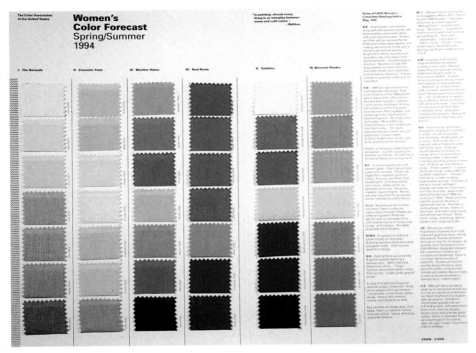

1. *Women's Color Forecast, Spring/Summer 1994. Courtesy of the Color Association of the United States.*

Since the founding of The Color Association of the United States in 1915, the avenues of color forecasting have steadily developed in size, range, and economic and social importance. As this century draws to a close, it seems appropriate that a worldwide group of professional color forecasters have been given the opportunity to present their views in this book by Professor Harold Linton.

For the first part of the twentieth century, color forecasters worked largely within national boundaries. For instance, the first American forecasting organization, The Textile Color Card Association of America (TCCA), predecessor of The Color Association of the United States (CAUS), was organized as a nation's response to the outbreak of World War I. Faced with the reality of being cut off from fashion information from Paris, presidents of leading American textile firms decided to coordinate their color approach. The result was *The Standard Color Reference of*

America, a book showing color standards for the wool, cotton, and silk industries in the United States. This reference showed 106 shades on silk ribbons that were based on nature's flora and fauna, college and university colors, and U.S. Armed Forces shades. Now in its Tenth Edition, the number of colors shown has approximately doubled. This proliferation of color underscores a global tendency that has greatly complicated the work of color forecasters.

The TCCA's first actual forecast, issued in 1917, focused on supplying appealing colors for women's clothing and accessories (gloves, hats, and hosiery). Today, women's fashion forecasts continue to be seminal. A clothing shade that is chosen for a select few one year, five years later tends to be favored by many and applied to a broad range of related products from activewear to leather goods.

To encourage acceptance of the Association's projected shades among industry professionals, a

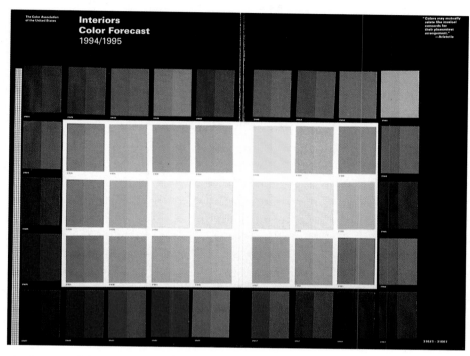

2. *Interiors Color Forecast, 1994/1995. Courtesy of The Color Association of the United States.*

forecast format was developed with designers and stylists very much in mind. The overall look and the interaction of various colors with one another were recognized. Appealing color groupings or combinations, intuitively understood by designers, also became the means of seduction by which others in nonfashion industries accepted subjective shade selections. An aesthetically pleasing forecast tends to look reliable and by dint of its appeal become a self-fulfilling prophecy. In other words, what is believed tends to become true in color forecasts, just as it does in economic ones.

In the aftermath of World War II, developing technologies in various consumer-oriented industries, such as automotive and packaging, realized the advantages of using colors that had proved their popularity in fashion industries. With the right red or green, one had a definite advantage. In the same postwar industrialization, fashion moved from the rooms of the couturier

and seamstress to the ready-to-wear racks of department stores. "Mass-marketing," or selling the same garment or goods to many people, began; the role of color forecasting assumed greater economic significance.

The Color Association of the United States kept pace by introducing other forecast cards. Separate, specialized forecast cards for man-made fibers were added in the 1950s; menswear color cards were issued in the 1960s; home furnishings were projected in the 1970s; and by the 1980s interior and environmental color palettes were published. Finally, in the mid-1980s cards geared to American children and to burgeoning activewear industries were published (figs. 1–2).

These special forecasts reflected the indisputable fact that color availability for most man-made goods—items ranging from electronics to artificial silk flowers—has increased with each decade. If a product line in 1930 used three colors, it was likely in 1980 to include a dozen or more. Given the proliferation of shades, the increasing sophistication of color technologies, and the ever-increasing demand by consumers for new colors each season, the Association's (and other) forecasts are even more important as an industry forum, both to supply and to coordinate new color ideas. As markets expand, they also begin to have a global significance, providing guidance on how colors will perform in different regions.

Today, The Color Association of the United States continues to enlist the volunteer efforts of industry professionals in reaching a consensus. Chair of the Men's Forecasting Committee, Jim Siewert, manager Trend Direction Hoechst Celanese, offered these remarks on the future of color in fashion:

> As we move forward into the next century there will be numerous strides made in the fashion world. Obviously, fabric and fiber technology, silhouette change, and day-to-day activities will be important considerations. However, most important will be color. The thousands of options in hue and degree of saturation will continue to be a major consideration in color. No matter what changes occur around us, the ability of color to alter moods, reflect personality, and change one's outlook will continue to be of utmost importance.

Textile designer Jack Lenor Larsen serves as chair of the CAUS Interior Forecasting panel. He foresees color forecasting's future this way:

> Because color forecasting works (it is, after all, self-fulfilling) we shall see more of it—but it will, necessarily, be more focused. Take my field of interiors: CAUS came up this year with the best card ever. Still, the fault lies in the breadth of the market covered, catering both "to the trade only," from top to bottom, and to the various important middle markets. Even these have regional/urban differences, and more importantly, there are the various aspects of contract vs. home furnishings to be considered. Contract includes hospitality and health care, which are more or less residential and user-friendly, vs. corporate offices, which are less colorful. But even within the home there are enormous differences between bed and bath, for instance, and the public

sectors. Consumers will take higher risks in selecting the color of their towels as compared to the living room rug or upholsteries. This is partly because they have several sets of towels and any mistakes can be easily passed on or left in the linen closet. They are ultra-conservative in those pieces that cannot be so hidden and could be open to criticism.

> I feel that, at least in furnishings, we could do better to earmark those colors which we feel are "forecast" or a high style, those we are confident in, and those that continue.

Mr. Larsen's comments on likely future specificity in forecasts and in their application bring us to Harold Linton's book, *Color Forecasting: A Survey of International Color Marketing.* Just as television stars and newscasters have themselves become subjects of televised programs, so color forecasting and the burgeoning field of color luminaries and councils are now a book. More importantly, this book is testimony to the international interest and openness of color specialists in sharing their insights on the ever-evolving and intriguing field of color forecasting.

MARGARET WALCH
ASSOCIATE DIRECTOR
THE COLOR ASSOCIATION OF THE UNITED STATES

Preface

This book is about and largely written by color forecasting and color marketing experts who are a network of professionals working together to turn color into meaningful information that is used by a wide assortment of business and service industries. Whether it is advanced color information, interpretation of past color movements, the interplay of design and color, or new solutions to current color problems, professionals from virtually every industry have a common commitment to color as the ultimate marketing tool and a belief that sharing noncompetitive information can reap positive benefits.

The Color Marketing Group® and The Color Association of the United States are the largest color marketing associations in the world, with many similar groups found in most countries, all of which are listed in the back of this book. The Color Marketing Group has more than 1300 international members. Color decision makers from every design profession, including color technicians, marketers, designers, stylists, merchandisers, managers, researchers, scientists, educators, and artists find so much information from these organizations in the form of published newsletters and literature, annual meetings, and lectures. Participation in these associations helps members make better color decisions that translate into profitable business ventures.

Color decisions are rarely made independently from other businesses. Professionals draw on information from domestic and international markets relating to color technology, color theory, demographic regional, and marketing influences. To aid members, The Color Marketing Group, as one example, offers regional, national, and international meetings, which include panel discussions, seminars, and a strong emphasis on participation in various workshops, roundtable discussions, and serious exchange of information. Sessions are usually lively exchanges between professionals from every field on such topics as future color directions, color marketing, and design. Special regional meetings, held at various times of the year, delve more deeply into topics of shared importance to the membership.

The resources, background research, and seminal thinking that color marketing and forecasting experts bring to bear on their field has been a subject not widely published nor well understood among design professionals and the public. This book offers a window into the nature of the profession—its development and growth, centers of research, dynamic organization, and the function and role of color marketing and forecasting in design, business, domestic and foreign cultures. Many practitioners from around the world have lent samplings of their work in an effort to share with the readership a glimpse into the disciplines and dealings of their professional practices. Often personal, lively accounts intertwined with notes on experience and business acumen reflect the hybrid nature of their activities in marketing and forecasting. Coming from such varied educational backgrounds as the arts, business, service industries, and many other disciplines, these individuals have defined circuitous pathways into practicing their art. Each is inevitably enriched by a diversity of background and preparation, and simultaneously finds the sharing of a breadth of professional exposures to be a refreshing and enriching resource for information. To them, collectively, I am indebted.

I have admired the wealth of information, creative savvy, and ability to communicate the many nuances of the language and practices of color design and graphic communication that Tom Porter brings forth in numerous journals, lectures, books, and on film. His willingness to offer preliminary advice on this book and his assistance with its vibrant introduction is deeply appreciated. I am grateful to Margaret Walch, Associate Director of The Color Association of the United States, for creating a thoughtful and reflective foreword for this project. I am also appreciative of Nancy A. Burns, CAE, Executive Director of The Color Marketing Group, and Kathleen M. Register, Director of Member Services, for their support with numerous constructive suggestions to the vast network of human resources that make up the membership of The Color Marketing Group association. I am simultaneously thankful to Patricia Verlodt, president of The Color Marketing Group, for her wonderful work on behalf of this book in reviewing material adapted from CMG literature; for a generous overview of CMG; and for a thoughtful essay on her own work, Color Services, Inc. Leatrice Eiseman introduced me to The Color Marketing Group, which, in turn, has provided abundant resources for this work—I am grateful to her for opening this door and for her well-recognized talents as a colorist and color authority.

Many contributors have shared their experiences reflecting on the nature of professional practice to help make this project a meaningful and sensitive view of a complex and highly diversified industry. A willingness to explain the attributes of research, planning, business, personal vision, visual and artistic skills necessary for success in each of the contributor's approaches (without divulging inappropriate corporate identities or aspects of strategic planning) is an act of faith that is deeply appreciated and reflected in the organization of the work.

My friends and colleagues, Mr. Shigenobu Kobayashi, president of the Nippon Color and Design Research Institute, Inc., and Ms. Setsuko Horiguchi, have my thanks for their support and generous contribution. Dr. Leonhard Oberascher has generously lent elements of his marvelous research into consumer color preferences in Europe. Jean-Philippe Lenclos has contributed an expansive survey of the far-reaching work of his Atelier 3D Couleur in Paris. I met Jacqueline Montgomery at the Fashion Institute of Tech-nology and was inspired by her presentation of the Oscar de la Renta Color Collection. She has written a memorable article about the Color Room entitled *History, Resource and Inspiration*. Giovanni Brino of Italy has shared with me his ground-breaking work with urban color restoration and forecasting for historic cities and regions in Europe and beyond. I am grateful for his view on forecasting colors from the past to the present in architecture. And to many new acquaintances, I have enjoyed our relationships and wish to personally acknowledge your patience and perseverance for an admirable effort in writing and organizing the materials for the book. My thanks to Elke Arora, Pauline Ashworth, AV Photographic, Everett Brown, Don Campbell, Diane Calvert,

Kenneth X. Charbonneau, Pierre Cardin, Robert S. Daily, Uri Feldman, Ellen Fideri, Greenpeace, Inc., Richard Herbert, Christine Hilke, J.A.F.C.A., Darlene Kinning, Michelle Lamb, Merle Lindby-Young, Michael Manwaring, David McFadden, Thad McIlroy, Pantone, Inc., Barry Ridge, Sue Ross, Maruchi Santana, Jacob Suchard AG, Sydney A. Sykes, Deborah Szwarcé, Patricia Tunsky, Alison Webb, Kay Stephenson Wrack, Electronics for Imaging, Paramount Pictures, White Reproductions, and Irene Zessler of PECLERS PARIS.

Finally, these projects did not happen without the support of several who remained behind the scenes but were vital to this book's success. Wendy Lochner, Senior Editor, Architecture, Van Nostrand Reinhold Company, has helped me to bring several projects to light—her wizardry and skills are abundant and deeply appreciated. Thanks to Sherrel Farnsworth, Donn Teal, and David Levine for their sensitivity toward the manuscript and Leeann Graham for her skill and care throughout the production. I have great admiration for my teaching colleague, Gretchen Rudy, who has shared in the development and organization of several of my books with careful guidance and criticism. My studio associates, Beth Boji and Mat Coates, have been invaluable support on all aspects of graphic design and preproduction. My thanks also to Diane Primrose, Anne Marie Corcos, and Galit Zolkower for clear and efficient translations of several articles from French to English. Saving the best for last, I give myself another opportunity to share with my wife and children the enjoyment of producing a companion book to my previous work, *Color Consulting*, and in doing so sharing our growing love.

HAROLD LINTON

Introduction
Color in the Looking Glass
*Tom Porter**

Many fashion industries, such as clothing, beauty, and cosmetics, depend heavily upon our constantly shifting color tastes for their existence. Indeed, their survival in the marketplace hinges upon the accurate forecasting of tomorrow's trendsetting colors. To service this need, each branch of these industries holds its own international fair, which draws together color predictions from a variety of sources. One such fair, Premier Vision, is held annually in Paris. This addresses particularly the textile industry and functions as a crystal ball in which future color trends are formulated from consultations between European forecasters. Once determined, the colors are then displayed on large presentation boards in the Hall of Prediction.

Similar consultations between experts in different fields occur all over the world. In England, for instance, there is the Color Group, which is affiliated with the Chartered Society of Designers in London. The Color Group represents a panel of representatives from different industries, including automotive, plastics, and paint, and whose deliberations act as a filter of information. Their color predictions are compiled under topical issues or themes, a representative palette of the following year's colors being culled from each sub-palette. Techniques of prediction used involve a streetwise approach, i.e., visiting the key international trade fairs, an analysis of recurrent

3. *Courtesy of Paramount Pictures.* The Great Gatsby
*Copyright © 1992 by Paramount Pictures. All Rights
Reserved.*

hues found in design magazines, and colors associated with successful museum exhibitions, or with box-office success in the theater and the cinema, etc.

The cinema particularly can exert a powerful influence on color fashion, and it is one that is recognized by many leading designers. For example, in the early 1970s the film *The Great Gatsby* launched the pinks and whites of the "Gatsby look" (fig. 3). It also launched the fashion designer Ralph Lauren to international recognition. Today, it is not unusual to find leading international fashion designers involved directly in major feature movies. Jean Paul Gaultier coincided his 1989 summer collection with the same costumes he designed for Peter Greenaway's *The Cook, The Thief, His Wife and Her Lover,* while Cerutti was responsible for the wardrobe designs in *The Witches of Eastwick* and *Fatal Attraction.*

Other forecasting techniques can involve qualitative research, in which the market potential of a new product design and its colors are evaluated directly with potential customers. One such group is Scantest Limited. They use a strict interview format in order to provide an accurate determination of the market for any given color or color range. In the first instance, this process is essentially one of color elimination, but later results are fed into a computer program that claims to provide forecasts of sales for certain colors. Product manufacturers can then review these findings prior to making any final color decision.

However, a more intuitive forecasting process takes place directly at street level. For instance, Sally Forbes, the fashion predictor, will make regular visits to Camden Market in London to simply observe new color trends possibly developing at street level. Other British color forecasters are known to take up similar vantage points in such cities as Paris. Yet another technique has been adopted by the French colorist Jean Philippe Lenclos. His method includes the regular monitoring of color on billboards, at motor shows, and in the display windows of selected fashion and furniture stores in Paris, London, Tokyo, and New York.

It was from Lenclos's international survey that, in the early 1980s, he detected a fusing of color fashion. Despite the fact that color cycles hitherto had moved at different speeds for different industries (fashions for clothes were about two years ahead of those for the home), a new phenomenon involving the unification of color trends had begun to emerge—one Lenclos describes as a "color revolution." This synchronizing of the speed of color cycles was also endorsed by the American color consultant Leigh Rudd Simpson. In 1989 she confirmed that color trends were driven by clothes fashion, and added: "When a color comes into fashion and is accepted by the customer, they respond by wanting to see that color all around them—in interiors, cars, graphic design, etc."

However, my own work in color forecasting stems from my study of the Victorian designer Owen Jones and his coloration of Joseph Paxton's Crystal Palace in 1851. In defense of his selection of rich, bright primary colors for its interior decoration, he cited the similar hues used architecturally by the ancient Greeks and described them as signals of highpoints in the development of a culture. Jones's comment alerted me to the fact that throughout history the cycling of color predilection has returned occasionally to a preoccupation with full-blooded primary hues. These points in time seem to reflect a need to return to color basics, i.e., moments in our history when we needed to rediscover color and to begin again. At these cyclical moments, we revel again in the power of reds, blues, and yellows before moving on into an ensuing exploration of the admixture. These historical points are found in the brilliance of Jones's colors and, indeed, in the work of many of his European contemporaries. They are found again in the beginning of the twentieth century in the pioneer paintings of Piet Mondrian, and later in the fabulous colors of Art Deco.

Such historical moments are in part fueled by a parallel and developing technology, as well as a mood of the time. For instance, approximately ten years after the opening of the Crystal Palace, William Henry Perkin launched his new aniline-based purple dye on a Victorian fashion world. Quickly joined by a strong and synthetic red, as well as a green dye, purple caused a sensation in women's clothing and created the "mauve decade." A further recycling of saturated color, again in the context of fashion clothing, came in the 1930s when Elsa Schiaparelli stunned the fashion world with her "shocking pink."

This relationship between our fascination with new color experiences and technology continues even in our color-saturated world of today. This search for color novelty has seen the multi-colored Swatch wristwatch and the colorizing of black-and-white Hollywood movie classics. Our obsession with surface color dazzle is also expressed in the iridescent holograms of our credit cards and in the dawning technology of a glass and a paint that will alter its hue on command.

Just beneath the surface of our adventure into different chromatic experience is another factor we should consider. This refers to the more consistent pattern of color aesthetics—first researched significantly in 1941 by Hans Eysenck. He had found a consistent order of color preference in adults—and described this order as the universal scale of color. Many tests have since been conducted, including several by the writer, which arrive at the same or similar results. Indeed, there is even evidence that this order is also preferred by rhesus monkeys—a finding that led its author, Dr. Nicholas Humphrey of Cambridge University, to suggest that this color scale is biologically based.

Eysenck's universal scale is as follows: 1. Blue; 2. Red; 3. Green; 4. Purple; 5. Yellow; and 6. Orange. The preference for blue crops up in a recent survey by *The Pulse*, the newsletter of the American Roper Organization, where almost fifty percent of those tested named blue as their favorite color, with red in second place. Blue is also America's best-selling car color, with red cars in second place. Meanwhile, Britain's top auto manufacturers identify blue, red, and white as consistently holding the inside track to the top sales positions. The popularity of blue also surfaces in some unusual products. For example, its preference can even challenge our known aversion

4. *Smarties. Courtesy of Tom Porter.*

5. *Smarties. Courtesy of Tom Porter.*

to blue foodstuffs. One color preference test involving various products and contexts (Porter, 1979) discovered the popularity of the blue Smartie (a range of colored candy similar to M&Ms). For the test, Rowntree Mackintosh prepared a special range of Smarties in Eysenck's six hues—each being controlled along the dimensions of value and chroma. The blue Smartie proved an outstanding success and was preferred far more than the other colors in the test. Although Rowntree Mackintosh did not produce a blue version at that time, they introduced one in 1987. Their blue was more intense than the one used in the test; however, the official blue Smartie was a huge success and proved itself more popular than all the other colors in their range (figs. 4–5).

The widespread popularity of blues and reds in certain contexts reinforces my firm belief that our color preference lurks just beneath the veneer of an ever-changing color fashion. Moreover, this preference becomes suppressed when the public mood is motivated toward a different color expression. For example, the British preference for blue, red, and white automobiles was suddenly overtaken in the early 1990s by a huge demand for British Racing Green—a color need that coincided with acute awareness of environmental pollution. Therefore, rather than expressing a nostalgic revival of the color associated with the heyday of British motor racing, this color choice reflected the conscience of society. But fashion can also reflect such moods as aspiration and fascination. This can be demonstrated if we survey the basic color trends of the last four decades.

6. *Men's fashion, 1968, by Pierre Cardin (model: Yoshi Takata). Courtesy of Pierre Cardin.*

The 1960s

This decade opened with a fascination for black, white, and metallic neutrals. These were expressed in the fashions of the period, including those from the design houses of Cardin, Courrèges, and Quant. Meanwhile, fine art was engaged in the scientific study of optical illusions—Op Art confining itself to the disturbance caused by visual fields using intense and geometric combinations of black and white. This mania for achromatics was, of course, a direct reflection of a science fiction fantasy—a recurrent theme is fashion and product design in which we become bedazzled by the glitter and gadgetry of black and silver electronic products. Indeed, the mathematical and hard-edged mood of the first part of the decade simply responded to the advent of space travel and our mental journey into outer space (fig. 6).

Meanwhile, the second half of the 1960s witnessed a complete change in our color mood. This followed the birth of the package holiday in Great Britain, the possibility of cheap travel to faraway places coinciding with a thirst for the experience of other cultures. Consequently, the bright organic hues of ethnic folk cultures entered the British home. Much of this color display focused on Indian culture, an interest that recycled an earlier focus on ancient Egyptian decoration, which in the 1930s had followed the discovery of Tutankhamen's tomb. However, this half of the decade also saw the emergence of the hippie and an hallucinogenic drug-inspired psychedelia that represented our journey into the inner space of our mind.

The 1970s

The 1970s saw our return to a science fiction fantasy but this time expressed in an exposed technology. We became deeply interested in how things worked. The need to confront the working parts of a complex technology saw visible mechanisms, such as exposed wristwatch

7. *Centre Pompidou in Paris, France. Courtesy of Tom Porter.*

architecture where the hitherto hidden working parts of buildings became exposed—their mechanical guts being spilled directly into the street for all to see. Perhaps the most famous example of the time, the Centre Pompidou, opened in Paris (fig. 7). However, this adventure into a high technology had to be clarified. To do so, bold primary and secondary colors were enlisted to diagram individual elements and the concept of "color-coding" had arrived. These "high tech" expressions of black, white, and the bold primary colors were also found in fashion and product design, where the influence of a revival of interest in the work of De Stijl designers brought slabs of red, black, blue, and yellow to our lifestyles.

The 1980s

The early 1980s saw a new mood which, albeit short-lived, accompanied an economic boom. This triggered the beginning of the "pastel phase," i.e., a period when fashion hues became mixed with white to represent "upmarket" and "sophisticated taste." Pastel colors spread quickly and became associated with lifestyle—a concept that involved various groups of colors aimed at different attitudes or fantasies of living, such as "nostalgia," "natural," "sporty," "classic," and "ethnic." Subdued color ranges became coordinated across all kinds of products associated with a particular "style of living," from clothes to cars and from interiors to luggage.

Fed by such popular television programs as the highly influential "Miami Vice," the pastel trend became truly international in spirit. For example, the coordinated hues of men's and women's clothing in New York in 1985 appeared in the same year and in the same colors for new automobile models launched at the Frankfurt, Paris, and Tokyo Motor Shows. Colors hitherto considered suitable only for baby clothes were worn by adults and were even used on Parker Pens and aggressive machines like Honda motorcycles and Fiat cars (fig. 8).

However, this quest for status through color was also tinged with a nostalgia for the past.

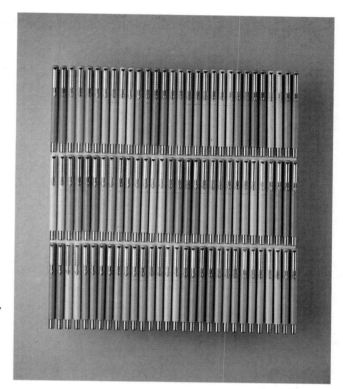

8. *Parker Pens 1985. Courtesy of Atelier 3D Couleur/Jean-Philippe Lenclos. Parker Pens, International, commissioned Atelier 3D Couleur to define the color palettes of the Vector pen destined for the European market. Three ranges were proposed. A study of the market permitted a verification of the predictions, and among the three proposed ranges they opted for this range of five grey-tinted colors, which achieved a resounding commercial success on all of the European markets. Courtesy of Atelier 3D Couleur/Jean-Philippe Lenclos.*

The search for "real bread" and "real ale" was embedded in the concept of an idealized rural life and a "cozy country cottage" style—a need being fed by the fashion and interior designs of Laura Ashley, Conran's Habitat, and Next. The "natural" theme also saw the success of Imperial Chemical Industries' Natural Whites, a range of white paint tinted with a hint of color. There was also the rise of "Muffin," a soft beige pastel that became Britain's best-selling paint color (after white) of the decade.

An international expression of pastel colors was stimulated by the painted facades and interiors of the Post-Modernist reaction to the drabness of a Modernist creed. Highly influential were the more figurative designs of Michael Graves, whose Mediterranean palette became transposed to product and electronic goods. This color mood was quickly adopted in the Japanese electronic industry, which launched pastel-pink televisions, powder-blue telephone handsets, soft grey and yellow transistor radios, as well as steam irons highlighted in pale yellow, blue, and pink.

The 1990s

News of the discovery by British scientists in 1987 of a hole in the earth's ozone layer had sunk into the public conscience by the end of the 1980s. Issues such as deforestation, global warming, and chemical pollution caused a deep concern for the future of the planet. By functioning as the watchdog of this deterioration, the hue of the Green Movement became the target of high fashion (fig. 9). While this color association found "responsible" yet gullible reactions to environmental awareness—green representing lead-free gasoline and the previously mentioned ascendancy of the green-colored automobile—green had become adopted again as the symbol of survival. This was simply an updating of the fertility hue found in antiquity, from the green-painted floors of ancient Egyptian temples to symbolize the fertile meadows of the Nile, to the myths of the Green Man and the Lincoln Green of Robin Hood.

The age of "greenness" has also started to modify traditional color meanings. It was predicted

9. *Greenpeace Literature/Logo. © Greenpeace, Inc. Courtesy of Greenpeace, Inc.*

in 1990 that white—traditionally associated with the packaging of such refined white foodstuffs as salt, flour, and sugar—would be replaced by earth brown, in reaction to the disturbing environmental effect of chlorine bleaching. However, by 1991 the "back to nature" fashion saw earthy browns, terra-cottas, golds, and silvers accompanying moss greens, grass greens, and leaf greens widely used in interior and product design.

As we move on through the 1990s, our quest for survival has demanded environmentally safe pigments and dyes for the more variegated and chromatically adventurous color ranges that have followed the green phase. However, several forecasters predict a return to the science fiction dream in the years immediately preceding the year 2000. In other words, a renewed interest in the subdued hues of blacks, greys, grey-blues, and grey

red-blues will hallmark the dying years of the present decade. This seems to point to nothing more than a pause in neutral before the onset of the next century—a lull before the storm of exuberance and innovation that is bound to accompany the thrust into the new millennium. After all, we still live today in the wake of the shock waves triggered by the exhilaration in design at the beginning of the twentieth century!

However, by looking back in order to peer into the future, this approach is necessarily broad in scope. Obviously, there are countless sub-plots (i.e., smaller eddies and currents of color trend, which are detected on a season-to-season basis within the larger waves of predilection). For instance, in focusing on color trends in interior design with particular reference to paint, my work has involved the monitoring of seasonal paint color sales as one means of plotting the rise and decline of individual hues. But this has always been conducted within the broader approach, which will differ from the many methodologies described in this book. However, within each branch of the manufacturing industries, each process of color prediction aims for the same result. Indeed, as these industries rely upon accuracy of forecast for their survival so do forecasters rely on accuracy for theirs.

---

*Tom Porter is a consultant to the Imperial Chemical Industries in England and a long-standing member of the ICI Color Trends Panel. He is a Senior Lecturer in design and graphics at the School of Architecture, Oxford Brookes University, in Oxford, England. He has spent many years researching the subject of color preference and has published numerous papers, books, and public television programs on the subject. He also lectures and conducts workshops on color in the United States, United Kingdom, and Europe.

LINGE DE MAISON   REGIONALISME

LINGE DE MAISON   BASIC LUMINEUX

LINGE DE MAISON   COCOONING COSY

LINGE DE MAISON   COMPAGNIE DES INDES

LINGE DE MAISON   NEW BAROQUE

LINGE DE MAISON   ETHNIQUE MASCULIN

Part One
Centers for Color Research and Color Forecasting

Many countries throughout the world have color organizations and associations that perform vital roles for businesses in gathering information, and in conducting research, forecasting, and design and styling activities. Their memberships are largely composed of creative people who could be called stylists. They "style" or "color" a line of products (i.e., fashion, automotive, furnishings, and anything where color is important to the sales of an item). There are also members with technical, marketing, and sales backgrounds. Included in Part One is a sampling of a few of the most well-known centers for color forecasting research and services. Their nature and purposes vary—some are focused on color education and research, while others provide a dynamic range of education, forecasting, and styling services. A full listing of international color associations and organizations involved in color forecasting activities is provided in the back of this book.

History, Resource, and Inspiration

Jacqueline Montgomery

Because color is ephemeral, its documentation is essential. Verbal descriptions are often insubstantial and color memory elusive. The selection of color begins first with personal taste or subjective experience. Group consensus among designers and professionals, or among students who are working together, depends on give-and-take, a complicated process of selection and substantiation. The *Françoise de la Renta Color Room* at The Fashion Institute of Technology (FIT) provides access to thousands of color samples and to myriad possibilities for combining those colors. It is a unique resource and a place to research how color problems can be worked out.

The Color Room is a reference and resource room for color study and an integral part of The Museum at FIT. This museum houses the world's most comprehensive study collection of clothing and textiles and is available to the design community for an annual fee.

The Color Room was designed as an ongoing project for the development of specialized color resources to be used by the students at FIT, by designers from the textile, apparel, home furnishings, and related industries who are members of The Museum at FIT, and by visiting scholars. Since it opened in December 1985, the Color Room has more than lived up to its original purpose by expanding in both content and use.

The alchemy of this brightly lit room is enlivened by a 1950s Du Pont de Nemours color selector system designed for the automotive industry. The system, a wall of 3500 enamel color

10A. *Original palette development from fine art. Fashion, buying, and merchandising class, September 1992. Photo courtesy of Irving Solero, staff photographer.*

10B. *Color palette development from textiles in the Design Laboratory's collection, Spring 1991. Photo courtesy of Irving Solero, staff photographer.*

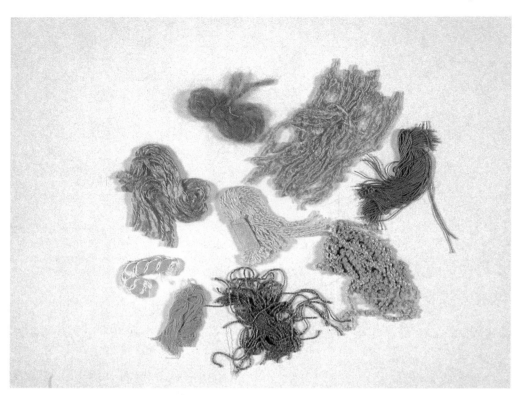

11A. *Color from the newly restored Sistine Chapel done with color from the Color Room by J. Montgomery. Photo courtesy of Irving Solero.*

11B. *Colors from the newly restored Sistine Chapel done with color from the Color Room by J. Montgomery. Photo courtesy of Irving Solero.*

chips, contributes to the creative energy of anyone who uses the room. Among the materials in the Color Room are examples of historic color cards from 1915 to the present for the apparel and home furnishings industries, various color systems, color reference books, color blankets and storyboards from *Mademoiselle* magazine's former semiannual fabric and color trend presentations. For students at the college, a continually updated selection of current forecasting material is also available.

The heart of the collection is housed in file cabinets flanking two walls of the Color Room: pieces of solid-colored fabrics and rug samples arranged by hue and value. Plastic containers above the cabinets contain smaller pieces of fabric, yarn, and leather samples. All these fabrics are selected for color only and not for their fiber content or structure. Designers, manufacturers, mills, and forecasting services generously donate samples on a continuous basis. These thousands of samples provide an instantaneous palette for the cutting, and are ready to be used by designers and students alike.

The actual task of filling and keeping the cabinets and bins well stocked is time-consuming and requires an educated understanding of color by the staff and student aides who sort out and file the swatches. For instance, what happens to yellow when it gets darker? It becomes olive green. And what happens to orange? It becomes brown. When colors are very greyed or dusty, which bin do they belong in? Color workshops and reference books are useful tools in helping students to answer these questions.

Designers, who use this facility as a privilege of Design Laboratory membership, can take samples of color to make up their own palette, find an elusive color shade, match color or pitch prints and woven patterns. Even designers or member companies who subscribe to forecast material themselves may still find the Color Room a useful supplement. Perhaps the fact that color direction has become both more enigmatic and also less unified or pervasive may be leading to more independent and eclectic color selection in general.

The classes that meet in the Color Room are in one- to three-hour workshops. Students learn first about the resources available to them and how to

research and utilize the collection for their class projects. Later, when they return to work individually, they are often assisted one-on-one.

Color workshops can augment the curriculum of classes in which color material is already an integral part, or the workshops may be an addendum. In either case, the additional color experience is helpful, especially when it takes place in an atmosphere where so much is readily at hand. The workshops do not take the place of semester-long, color-related courses offered at FIT. But for students who do not take a specific color course, it is a good place to learn some basics.

In the workshops, students are given an overview of color forecast services, what particular part of the market these services address, and their similarities and differences. Students are taught to look at color cards: They learn how to assess what they see, how to be articulate in expressing the quality of each color, or groups of colors, in terms of hue, value, and intensity. An important part of the training is developing the skill to observe the annual changes in the colors themselves and the ways in which they are combined. Other considerations are the significance of the color story or trend that is being conveyed, color naming, and how all the materials can be applied to designing or developing a line of merchandise for a specific customer.

On a broader scale, the importance and necessity for color change is discussed. Students in every aspect of design and merchandising must realize the visual power that color carries in appealing to and attracting the customer. This is especially true in a market where differences of silhouette may be minimal, and where economics has curbed individuality in detail, embellishment, and fabrication.

Students learn how to research or develop color palettes as professionals do, by going to primary sources. Color inspiration, as well as design or pattern—they are hard to separate—may come from fine or applied arts, architecture, or photography (figs. 10A–B). Often color direction is keyed to current painting or other important exhibitions taking place somewhere in the world (figs. 11A–B). The painter or artist who is not inhibited by commercial considerations is a risk

12. *Color story-board done by a student for a class in fashion art of Daria Dorosh. This project was not done in a Color Room workshop but was inspired by a project done earlier there. Photo courtesy of Irving Solero, staff photographer.*

taker. His or her vision, sometimes shocking, can transport us from the doldrums of preconceived notions of color and form.

Color is also influenced by political and cultural issues—the recent emergence of independent Eastern European states and the focus on conservation and ecology, popular films, rock groups, and street culture all provide ideas (fig. 12). We may look back to the 1960s, 1970s, and even 1930s for inspiration. Archival material, here the actual color cards from these periods, may be referred to.

Other workshops, sometimes in conjunction with teachers who bring their classes to the Color Room, include pragmatic problems of color theory for product development students, the recoloring of textile designs, an exercise in matching lab dips, an adaptation of a Johannes Itten problem in subjective color timbre expressing personal taste and feelings of harmony, and various slide presentations (fig. 13). The individual needs of the classes are discussed with their instructors beforehand, and often new approaches are tried.

Color workshops are meant to be fun. They

13. *Students in the Color Room working on Subjective Color Timbre project. Class is in textile science, coming for a warm-up and color inspiration. Photo courtesy of Irving Solero, staff photographer.*

allow students to use intuition and spontaneity in place of preconceived ideas of color, a "gestalt," or habitual use. Students who ponder such questions as "shall I use red with blue?" are instructed to go to the bins and let the colors talk directly to them and to see how one color looks next to another. With hundreds of reds to choose from, why waste valuable time conceptualizing?

Groups of foreign students and professionals have used the resources of the Color Room for workshops similar to those given to the students of FIT, with the specific purpose of increasing their understanding of the American market. The results have been equally rewarding for both the school and the recipients in promoting understanding of differences, as well as growing similarities, between cultures (figs. 14A–C).

Learning about color is subtly difficult. In a school that trains designers, color skills and sensitivity are essential. Most difficult of all is helping a student develop an individual and creative color vocabulary and expression. A good beginning for this personal exploration is the Color Room.

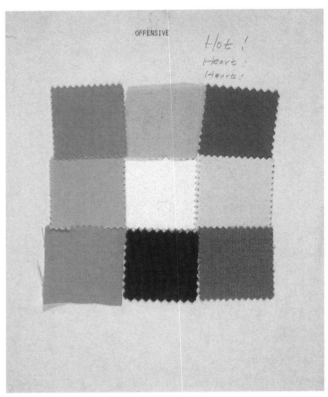

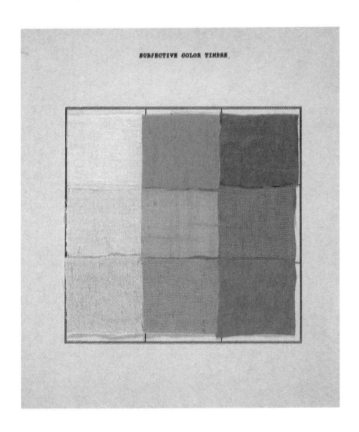

14A–C. *Subjective color timbre projects of Chinese designers. Their color sensibility is interesting and somewhat different from American students, June 1992. Photo courtesy of Irving Solero, staff photographer.*

Color Forecasting for Historical Cities and Regions

Giovanni Brino

The problem of restoring the painted facades of historical city centers in Europe has only been given systematic attention since the end of the 1970s. Since then, the first color plans have been carried out with the foundation of a specific urban restoration school, and the first facades colors data-banks have been set up in order to correctly forecast the historical colors on an urban and regional scale.

Color Prediction for Historical City Centers

The *Color Plan for Turin,* carried out by the writer between 1978 and 1983,[1] represents the first attempt in Italy at a rational response to the problem of restoring facades on a citywide scale on the basis of objective historical documentation. Its aim was to establish an operative color palette and a color map in a city where every year more than 1000 facades are normally repainted.

The color plan was born as an extension to the whole city of a research method applied for the first time at the end of the 1960s to the restoration of the neoclassical "Casa Antonelli" in Turin.[2]

1. Brino, G., and Rosso, F., *Colore e città: Il piano del colore di Torino, 1800–1850,* Idea Books Edizioni, Milan 1980, with English text (second edition: *Colore e città: I colori di Torino, 1801–1863,* Idea Books Edizioni, Milan 1987).

2. Brino, G., and Rosso, F., "La Casa dell'Architetto Alessandro Antonelli in Torino," *Atti e Rassegna Tecnica della Società degli Ingegneri e degli Architetti in Torino,* n. 5–8, 1972.

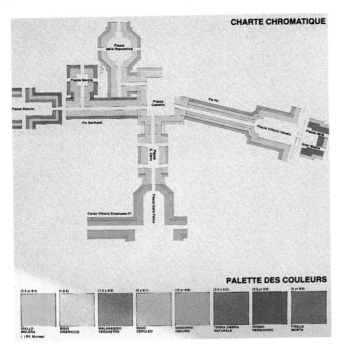

15A. *Colors prediction for the city center of Turin (north of Italy), based on historical archives documents: (left, top) color map of the main streets and squares; (left, bottom) color palette of the same streets and squares. Photos courtesy of Giovanni Brino.*

15B. *(right) Piedmont colors data bank. Photo courtesy of Giovanni Brino.*

This restoration was in fact based on accurate research into the archives, carried out with the collaboration of Franco Rosso, a specialist in the history of architecture and town planning in nineteenth-century Turin, which brought about the discovery and revival of the original color plan in 1970.

On the basis of historical research into the archives of the colors of Turin buildings, the discovery was made of an existing color plan of Turin, drawn up for the entire city by the Council of Architectural Advisors (Consiglio degli Edili) between 1800 and 1850. The Color Plan proposed by the author to the city of Turin in 1978 was intended to be a scientific reconstruction, with some adaptation, to the actual reality of the nineteenth-century color plan, being itself a rationalization of the color of some of the main streets and squares in the baroque period (fig. 15A).

The color palette has been distributed to all the producers, house painters, architects, and other professionals interested in house painting coded with the Munsell system of notation (fig. 15B).

The original historical colors having completely disappeared, the color palette, once painted directly onto the northern wall of the City Hall court, can now be considered as a forecasting tool for the producer, the house painter, and the owner, just as a color palette for the modern car industry, the textile industry, etc. The only difference is that the color palette for an ancient city is based on historical data, which can be found in the city archives or in original color samples tested by a chemical or physical laboratory.

In addition to the *Color Plan for Turin*, the author has drawn up a score of current color plans for various cities in Italy (in Piedmont, Lombardy, Liguria, Tuscany, Lazio, Abruzzo, Campania, and Sicily)[3] and in France (Mouans-Sartoux, near Cannes; Marseilles; and Estaque, the famous village of the artists' colony of the late nineteenth century).[4]

These color plans have stimulated two types of activity that have been integrated by the author

3. Brino, G., "Die Farbgebung historischer Stadtzentren in Europa," *Bauwelt*, n. 47, 1991.

4. Brino, G., Méthodes de Diagnostique, Banque de Données et Intervention, "Le Centre Historique de Marseille" (*Le Quartier Noailles*, n. 4, 1991; *Le Quartier du Panier*, n. 6, 1991; *Les Centres Villageois*, n. 7, 1991; *Le Quartier Belsunce*, n. 8, 1992; *Les Façades en enduit-ciment*, n. 10, 1992).

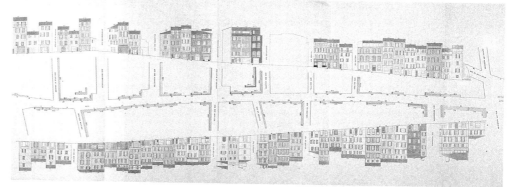

16A. *Color forecasting for the city of Marseilles (south of France), based on original color samples survey: (top) strip and color map of the* rue du Panier. *Photo courtesy of Giovanni Brino.*

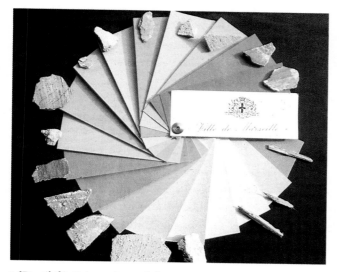

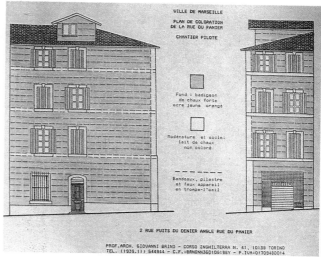

16B. *(left) Color palette of the same street. Photo courtesy of Giovanni Brino.*

16C. *(right) Color project of a facade chosen as a sample restoration with the related color palette. Photo courtesy of Giovanni Brino.*

whenever possible: professional training in the field of urban restoration (intended as a means to solve the practical problems connected with the use of traditional materials and techniques that disappeared for 50 years) and the data-banks of facade restorations, both at an architectural and at an urban and regional level (fig. 16A).

Color Forecasting and Professional Training in the Field of Urban Restoration

The desertion for over forty years of historical city centers and the consequent lack of maintenance of their legacy of buildings, caused the traditional materials with which the facades were originally painted (lime and colored earths) to disappear little by little, together with those craftsmen skilled

16D. *A detail of the facade after restoration. Photo courtesy of Giovanni Brino.*

in their application, making the correct realization of color plans difficult, and the historical colors forecasting inapplicable and unrealistic.

In order to solve the problem of the reuse of obsolete techniques and to acquire materials needed for the correct interpretation of the color palette, the Scuola di Restauro Urbano di Turino (Turin School of Urban Restoration) was established in 1982 under the direction of the writer. Professional training courses at an urban, regional, and EEC level were organized, involving exchanges of experience with other Italian regions, Switzerland, France, Spain, Portugal, and Germany.[5]

Together with this teaching and professional training activity, practical experimental work was developed with the establishment of a mobile workshop, which was able to be moved easily throughout Italy and other countries in order to survey specific restorations in contexts different from Turin[6] (fig. 16B).

This structure, which has been operative since 1983, has been staffed by a team of skilled craftsmen (decorators, masons, stucco decorators, and restorers) and has made it possible to carry out restoration work with traditional techniques and materials. By means of the mobile laboratory, it is possible to gather experience in restoring facades with dry lime and fresco in various Italian regions, as well as in France and Switzerland, adapting the work whenever possible to historical and local materials and techniques for a correct application to the color plans (figs. 16C–D).

Data-Banks of Facade Restorations at an Architectural, Urban, and Regional Scale

To facilitate the management of correct color forecasting, as the development of research into historical archives progressed concerning the color of facades in various Italian regions, carried out within the program of the Environmental Design course directed by the writer in the School of Architecture at Turin Polytechnic and the experience of color plans and professional training, a system of gathering and processing data on the restoration of facades has been put into operation.

The first data-bank of this type was the Colors Data-bank of Turin.[7] Little by little, for each color plan carried out, along with the experience of professional training described above, a data-bank based on specially designed charts of colors of facades, found from research into archives or based on original color samples surveyed directly in the historical facades, was put into operation.

By means of continually improving this system of gathering and processing data, the insertion of graphic images and photographs of the facades concerned was achieved via videodisc, as in the case of the data-bank for the facades of Marseilles.[8]

The data-bank system has been extended to a regional scale, with the Data-bank for Colors in Piedmont[9] and the Data-bank for Trompe-l'oeil Painted Facades in Liguria,[10] including experimental verifications of sample restoration of painted facades (fig. 16A).

5. Ibid., "La scuola di restauro urbano di Torino," *Acclaim* (Turin), 1988 (with English text); Ibid., "Restauration urbaine et formation professionnelle," *Les jeunes et le patrimoine architectural: Travaux réunis à l'issue du colloque organisé à Paris à l'Unesco en 1989*, Liège: Mardaga, 1990.

6. Ibid., "Il laboratorio mobile per il restauro delle facciate," *Bollettino di Italia Nostra*, n. 266, June 1989.

7. Brino, G., "Applications de l'informatique à la couleur et au mobilier urbain," *Actes de la 7e Conférence Européenne sur la CFAO et l'Infographie*, Paris, Hermès: 1988; Ibid., "Applications of the Computer to Color and Street Furniture," Lisbon: 13th Urban Data Management Symposium, 1989; Ibid., "Constitution d'une banque de données des façades à Turin," *Métiers et Patrimoine-Revue du Conseil de l'Europe*, Supplement, June 1990; Ibid., "Turiner Farbgebung durch Farbendatenbank erstellt," *Farbe & Raum*, n. 2, 1991.

8. Brino, G., and D., "Constitution d'une banque de données de savoir-faire. Le quartier du Panier à Marseille," *Métiers du Patrimoine-Revue du Conseil de l'Europe*, February 1990.

9. Brino, G., *Colori e territorio: La banca dati dei colori del Piemonte*, Idea Books Edizioni, Milan, 1985 (with English text).

10. Ibid., *Colori di Liguria: Introduzione ad una banca dati delle facciate dipinte liguri*, Genova: Sagep Editrice, 1991; Ibid., *I colori di Noli: Dal piano del colori al cantiere pilota*, Genova: Sagep Editrice, 1992.

17A. *Color forecasting for the city of Subiaco (Western Australia), based on original color samples survey: (top) detail of the facades strip and color map of Rokeby Road. Photo courtesy of Giovanni Brino.*

17B. *(middle, left) Historical photo of the Subiaco Hotel with the original red brick facade with the "tuck-pointing" treatment. Photo courtesy of Giovanni Brino.*

17C. *(middle, right) Existing symbolic/commercial color scheme (the facades have been painted in green, white, and red, like the Italian flag). Photo courtesy of Giovanni Brino.*

17D. *(bottom, left) Two options of restoration project of the same facade: with painting imitating the original brick and stone color or with the recovery of the natural bricks and stones. Photo courtesy of Giovanni Brino.*

17E. *(bottom, right) Color palette of the existing color scheme of the Subiaco Hotel. Photo courtesy of Giovanni Brino.*

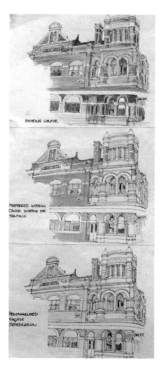

Recently, the same system was adapted to an architectural scale with the setting up of a data-bank on the restoration of the Villa Medici in Rome[11] for the French Ministry of Culture, based on archive documents dated between 1802 and 1968, including an experimental verification of the restoration of two shrines in the gardens of this villa, based on documents from the period and laboratory analyses.

The last application of the author's methodology of color forecasting in the historical centers has been made for the old district of Subiaco in Perth, western Australia[12] (figs. 17A–E).

11. Brino, G., and D., *The Restorations of Villa Medici in Rome, 1802–1968: An Operational Data Bank,* 14th Urban Data Management Symposium Proceedings, Odense, UMDS, 1991.

12. This experience has been made in cooperation with the Department of Design, Curtin University of Technology (Color, Communication and Environment Seminar, directed by Paul Green-Armitage).

Color and Image Forecasting

Color Forecasting to Predict Contemporary Images

Nippon Color & Design Research Institute, Inc.

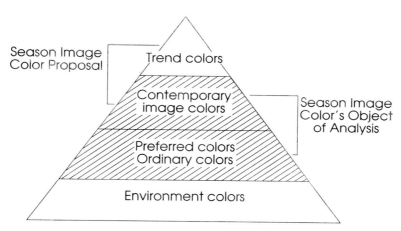

18. *Contemporary Image Colors. Courtesy of The Nippon Color and Design Research Institute, Inc.*

Since 1966, the Nippon Color and Design Research Institute has been analyzing contemporary taste by applying the psychology of color. In addition to color consulting, the Institute performs color forecasting as one of its many activities.

The Institute publishes the results of its color forecasting activities in a publication entitled *Season Image Color*. Issued twice yearly in April and October in a revised-format A4-size file book of approximately 90 pages, *Season Image Color* presents color forecast proposals for the forthcoming year. The book consists of two sections, one containing color forecast proposals and the other containing data representing the results of forecasting analyses. Since the start of its publication in 1981, over 20 issues have been released.

The Institute's color forecasting includes not only so-called trend colors, but also colors that characterize the image of the contemporary period. We believe the values that society regards as important are internalized by people as images, and prevail for two or three years as the contemporary image. The contemporary image color is the contemporary image expressed as color. A period could be characterized, for example, by bright or neutral colors.

Figure 18 provides a schematic representation of the method used by the Institute to identify colors. Please note how contemporary image colors are conceptualized in the diagram: The closer the color is to the base of the triangle, the more it resists change; the closer it is to the tip of the triangle, the more likely it will quickly go out of fashion.

The colors at the bottom are the "environment colors," meaning the colors of the natural, social, and cultural environment. These include the colors of nature (sea, earth, vegetation) and the colors of an urban landscape. The colors on the level above are the "preferred colors" and "ordinary colors." Preferred colors refers simply to those that people like, which vary between men and women and type of lifestyle among other considerations. Ordinary colors are used with particular frequency in the commercial realm, for example, in lipsticks and in interior design. Trend colors are ones so designated by the Japan Fashion Color Association. These colors grow in popularity, as they are adopted by material and apparel manufacturers for use in their products. For example, if orange is forecast to be popular the following spring and summer, orange is a trend color.

There are several reasons why the Institute places emphasis on forecasting contemporary image colors. First, we try to create a color assortment that defines a general image covering a wide range of fields, including not only fashion, but also construction, interior design, and other products. We are thereby able to specify an appropriate color image for each field. From the trend color, moreover, we can identify the color that will be accepted by society with the least resistance and that will serve as the general basic color. Furthermore, in making forecasts, we always keep in mind the announced popular colors and incorporate these into our forecasts of contemporary image colors. This allows us to recommend the best way of exploiting the image color at the same time.

Methodology of Color Forecasting

Identifying contemporary images is the principal work of color forecasters. At the same time, it is important to identify the images represented by the color and design of current products and environments, as well as those preferred by the consumers who make up the contemporary market.

The Color Image Scale

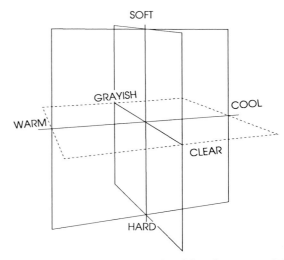

19. *The Color Image Scale. Developed by The Nippon Color and Design Research Institute, Inc., under Patent.*

The Color Image Scale[1] developed by this Institute is the most important tool in identifying the images of colors. This scale, developed from much color image research, allows images to be identified objectively. Single colors, adjectives, and color combinations expressed by these adjectives are arranged along coordinate axes representing a scale of warm-cool, soft-hard, and clear-greyish[2] (fig. 19).

The Color Image Scale may be applied not only to colors, but also to objects and phenomena. By examining the items' relative position and pattern formation on the scale, the analysis and evaluation of various images are possible (fig. 20).

By using this scale, the results of three types of trend analyses (i.e., contemporary scene, products and environment, and people) can be converted to images to determine which images are the most important. This step is the most significant from the standpoint of forecasting.

The specific methods employed are as follows (fig. 21):

---

1. Developed by the Nippon Color and Design Research Institute, Inc. Under Patent.

2. Kobayashi, S., "The Aim and Method of the Color Image Scale," published in *Color Research and Application*, Vol. 6, No. 2, Summer 1981. John Wiley & Sons, Inc.

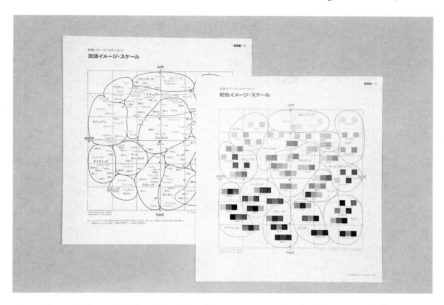

20. *Keyword Image Scale, Color Combination Image Scale. Courtesy of The Nippon Color and Design Research Institute, Inc.*

1. The analysis of current trends begins by gathering information from newspapers, magazines, and TV broadcasts on contemporary period, trends, fads, and popular products. Items that appear at first glance to be scattered or unrelated are analyzed, using the scale to check the distribution of their common images.

2. The analysis of products and environments consists of two parts. The first is market color analysis, which involves studying the colors of current products, such as men's and women's fashions, interior designs, home appliances, and automobiles. The second is image scale analysis of images associated with various established products. These include men's and women's fashions, interior designs, home appliances, and automobiles, and where appropriate, analysis of packaging, corporate images, and environments (fig. 22). The results of these analyses are then compared with the results of contemporary trend analyses to determine whether they agree in terms of the images identified. Last, the results are used to develop a lifestyle scene-

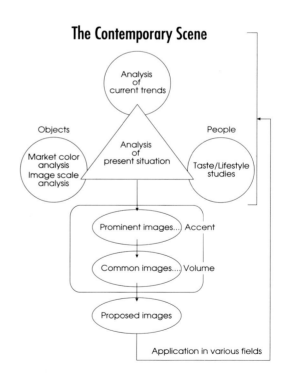

21. *The Contemporary Scene. Courtesy of The Nippon Color and Design Research Institute, Inc.*

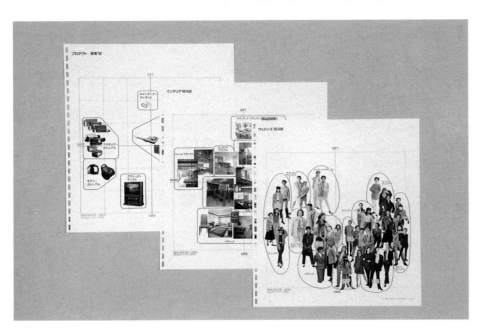

22. *Image Scale for various objects—Women's Fashions '92 AW, Interior Design '92 AW, Home Appliances '92. Courtesy of The Nippon Color and Design Research Institute, Inc.*

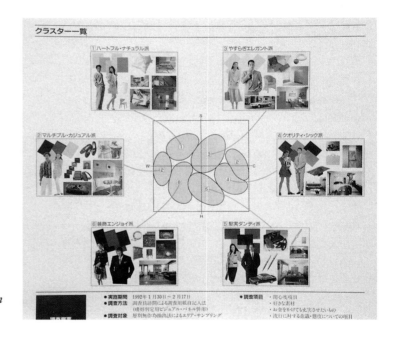

23. *Six patterns of taste/lifestyle. Courtesy of The Nippon Color and Design Research Institute, Inc.*

setting hypothesis to be part of the final proposal.

3. Research on people includes studying the degree of interest in or liking for certain images, and the study of tastes and lifestyles. Research into tastes and lifestyles is based on cluster analysis, in which taste is used as the criterion of classification (fig. 23). This method was developed by the Institute and differs from conventional lifestyle analysis based on classifications of attitudes and behavior. The index of classification used in the Institute's method is people's tastes in terms of color and design of living spaces, products, automobiles, and so on. The results are then collated with contemporary trend analyses to provide definitive materials on people's desired images. The results of the

24A. *The Image Visual and Image Color of "Northland." Season Image Color,* Vol. 23. *Courtesy of The Nippon Color and Design Research Institute, Inc.*

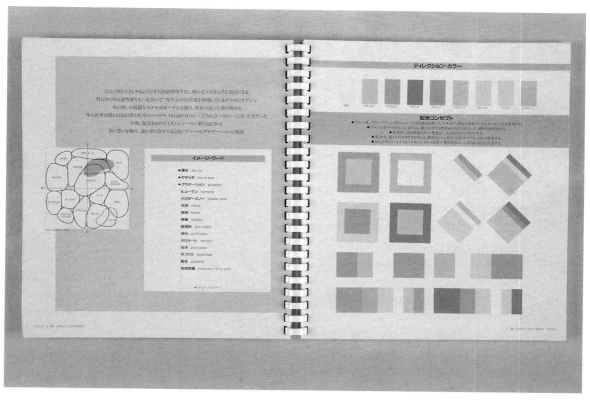

24B. *Image words and the color combinations used as the image colors for "Northland." Courtesy of The Nippon Color and Design Research Institute, Inc.*

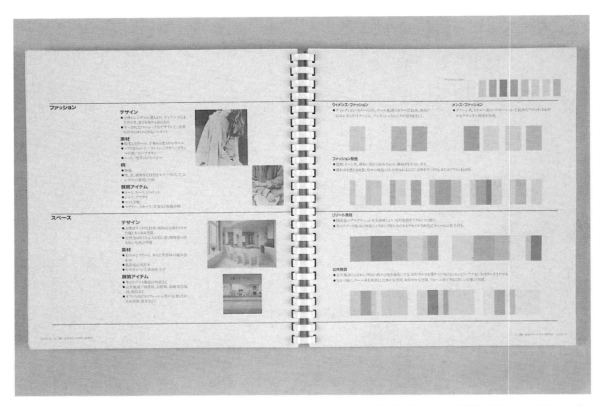

24C. *Examples of the application of the "Northland" image in various fields. Courtesy of The Nippon Color and Design Research Institute, Inc.*

above analyses are then gathered together on one of the image's scales. This enables us to understand the nature of the volume images and accent-type images currently in vogue. By comparing these with past results, moreover, it is possible to ascertain whether the currently popular volume images will remain popular, or whether their popularity will increase or decline. For accent-type images, we can identify those regarded as having charm or appeal and those whose popularity may increase in the future. Upon completion of these multifaceted studies, we can select our forecasted images for the following year. Because the forecasts relate to

the forthcoming year, it is also necessary to examine political and economic predictions, and to check on any upcoming important events, such as the Olympic Games. By applying data gathered over ten years of color forecasting related to cyclical changes in contemporary images, and of the images associated with particular periods, the Institute is able to prepare highly accurate forecasts.

The next step is to select colors that represent the images identified. Colors conforming to the images are selected in assortments of six to nine colors comprising a single image. The image scale is of great use here in clarifying the relationship between concepts (words) and colors.

Example of a Color Forecast Proposal

Two types of proposals are prepared for publication in *Season Image Color:* direction proposals for those that are highly predictive, and theme proposals. At the present time, three image forecast proposals are presented in each issue: one direction proposal and two theme proposals.

The example to be given here is the direction proposal for fall and winter 1993, namely the "Northland" image. This image is intended to impart a new sense of the charm and beauty of winter emerging from the natural environment and lifestyle of the north country. The background of this image is the continuing worldwide concern for ecology and the environment, and the image of the snow country that is part of Japan's identity. This image of freshness and relaxation is expressed in a soft emotional way using a gradation of cool greyish colors.

This type of image is presented by means of a total image visual presentation, the image color, a color combination using the image color, image words, and so on (figs. 24A–B). Specific color combinations and suggestions relating to their use are also offered for each specific field in which they are to be deployed (fig. 24C).

Season Image Color is currently distributed only to the roughly 300 member companies. The section on color forecast proposals is used by these firms for color planning, while the data section is used for product development, setting image concepts, and so on. Recently, foreign companies with established operations in Japan have become subscribers to the publication.

Color Marketing Group

Patricia Verlodt, President 1991–92

In 1963, a segment of the Inter-Society Color Council decided to address the issue of color as it related to marketing and The Color Marketing Group (CMG) was formed. In its early days, the group was small and mainly consisted of paint and textile industry members. They met to discuss various issues of color and network with similar industries for the exchange of information. As the group grew, so did its purpose and intent. The workshop experience has been a mainstay in the group, as it brings together members of similar products or end uses and allows for the exchange of market trends, forecast information, new technology, and a gamut of information invaluable to the marketplace. The greatest benefit of The Color Marketing Group is the opportunity it affords its members to exchange information. Because no product stands alone, each one is influenced by another product or area, and having such a diverse group of members and products represented at each conference allows this exchange to take place. Over 1000 companies are represented in CMG membership, and each conference draws about 500 of those members twice a year. Products and services in the CMG membership include consumer, commercial, residential, transportation, architectural/building, communications/graphics, fashion, retail, hospitality, office, health care, toys, recreation/sportswear, and textiles. The members themselves are designers, colorists, consultants, technicians, marketers, educators, and researchers.

25A. *Color Marketing Group Workshops. The Broadmore Hotel, Colorado Springs, Colorado. Photo courtesy of Bob McIntyre and DDF & M Public Relations.*

25B. *Same as above. Photo courtesy of Bob McIntyre and DDF & M Public Relations.*

Workshops

There is a place for each and every one of CMG's members in a workshop, from the forecaster to the technician (figs. 25A–B). Forecast workshops are restricted to those who forecast out two years or more, and they include Consumer Color Directions and Contract Color Directions. From these work-shops come the Color Directions palettes that are available to all members (fig. 26).

Those who select colors in a time frame of less than two years may attend Colors Current Workshops, as may others who do not forecast at all. Since these workshops address colors that are or will soon be in the marketplace, a knowledge of your own product comes to light in these workshops. A Colors Current palette is produced using the information gathered at these workshops. Since these workshops address current colors, they have the opportunity to track colors that were

26. *Color Marketing Group 1994 Colors. Photo courtesy of Patricia Verlodt.*

forecast for the current year at a previous conference. This tracking process validates the forecast palette and has proven the successful track record that Color Marketing Group has maintained for years.

Design Influences Workshops address all the influences of color. These workshops explore demographics, economics, or a specific design trend that makes color trends happen. A report is made to the entire membership as to the findings of this group.

Color Combinations Workshops include both Consumer and Contract members at different times of the year and explore the latest combinations and blends of colors in a myriad of

products. Since color rarely stands alone, this is an important part of the color experience. Mixed Workshops allow each workshop participant to receive information from other workshops and share his or her own workshop experience with others. This enables the broadest dispersal of information to the most members on a one-to-one basis. Marketing Workshops look into such issues as presentations and market research.

Since the fashion industry's time frame for seasons of color is different from those in other industries, the fashion members of CMG meet in the winter and summer with other members of the fashion community to develop a fashion palette. This palette is available to all members and is presented to the membership at each conference.

At each meeting distinguished speakers and color authorities make presentations to the membership. International trends, trade shows, fashion information, and reports are an integral part of CMG.

CMG produces *Color Directions,* which does not predict specific hues or shades but is rather an indication as to the direction color makes. CMG is so diverse that specific information is not possible but is left to the members' experience based on the palette.

Because CMG has a member base of over 1200 international members and each member is a part of the decision process in producing *Color Directions,* it is considered an extremely viable color source.

CMG's committees enjoy an uncommonly high level of participation, unlike many organizations and groups. Members serve on a variety of committees, including Graphics, Design, Education, Color Directions, Colors Current, Color Combinations, and International Color-Link. Working year-round on committee assignments, members grow both personally and professionally as their creative efforts advance the field of color marketing.

Atelier 3D Couleur: Trends, Signs, and Symbols

Jean-Philippe Lenclos

Today, fashion, design, and everyday products comprise a vast creative enterprise of objects and environmental images made to seduce and to sell. The industrial machine irresistibly manufactures products that are always adaptable to the target markets and to increasingly demanding customers. So the problematic components of success lie in the studios of creation, on the drawing tables, and in the headquarters of fashion, style, and design.

What dominant factors, when put together with sufficient lead time, will magically propel the dream object into the spotlight and best answer the consumer's expectations? Among the base parameters where forms, materials, and decor conspire, color is without a doubt the most evident, the most exultant, but also the most troublesome. Color is language, a form of expression, a system of signs and codes. Entrenched in traditions and cultures, it belongs to all; it is a vital element of the environment. The evolution of color can be analyzed, predicted, and quantified, but to what limits?

The customs of many diverse social groups are reflected in specific attitudes through color. These sociocultural behaviors are largely influenced by geological, climatic, regional, and national givens, where light plays an essential role determining attractions or rejections vis-à-vis certain tonalities or color associations. This we call "The Geography of Color."©

This vast nebula of trends and senses of identity belongs to the universe of cycles, where color is in continual evolution. How does one find one's way between that which belongs to authentic socio-

27. *1978—On the walls of Paris, the magazine* Elle *announces "the first trends of 1978." This poster is the first manifestation in urban space of the colors that will be in the spring fashions: "information, education, sensitivity." Color thus enters into the clothing language and into everyday life. Courtesy of Atelier 3D Couleur/ Jean-Philippe Lenclos.*

28. *April 1983—"Play the Style": the "Samaritaine" department store in Paris posts on the walls of the city the new concept of style in men's fashions. It is no longer only a question of fashion here, but of style and colors. Style is a way of life and color is chosen in harmony and coordination. Courtesy of Atelier 3D Couleur/Jean-Philippe Lenclos.*

29. *March 1984—"All of the Colors of the World." Benetton asserts the concept of colors. Basic writing of fashion and clothing. In social and international culture, color today is no longer a domain reserved for women, but is presented as co-ed: for men and women, same range and same visual language. Courtesy of Atelier 3D Couleur/Jean-Philippe Lenclos.*

cultural traditions and phenomenons of style provoked by chance societal occurrences, events, history, or pure creative invention of art?

Since the 1980s, we have witnessed the untimely multiplication of "trend notebooks" offered to industrial sectors of ready-to-wear, of home furnishings and decoration components, of sports articles, of decorative tableware (glasswork and dishes), and of automobiles! These predictions propose the keys to the best way to stick to the market, clarify the ideas, and facilitate the choices. But only to a certain point, for the overabundance of information and prefabricated definitions based on nothing at all risk drowning out the industrials

and provoking a withdrawal toward the standard and conformist formulas. The fundamental role of colorists or professional stylists remains, and they must find, across all these influences, their own operational conductive wire. This capability affirms by color the cultural senses of identity and advances toward the creation of a progressively better-educated public that is more open to color, modes of expression, and vectors of identity. These trends are nothing in themselves, and are only valuable on the condition of being signs and symbols, a supplement of the soul and a carrier of culture for quality of the frame of life (figs. 27–29).

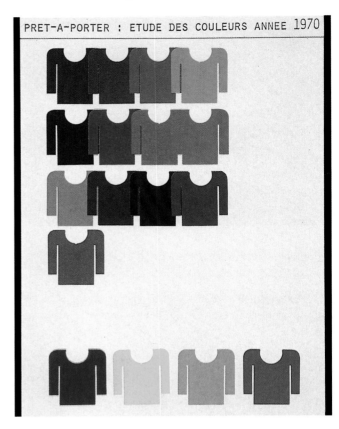

PRET-A-PORTER : ETUDE DES COULEURS ANNEE 1970

30. *1970—The synthesis of dominant colors in the ready-to-wear sector. Dominant blues, appearance of purple. Browns and earth tones. Four basic colors recall the influence of Op' Art from the 1960s. Courtesy of Atelier 3D Couleur/Jean-Philippe Lenclos.*

The Trends on Street Posters Predictions: Trends/ Mediatization of Colors

Color is a dynamic in enterprise development that is no longer possible to be arrived at in an empirical and arbitrary manner. Whether it concerns industrial products, household appliances, ready-to-wear clothing, or home interiors, trends will appear, fashions will be created and evolve. Some trends are ephemeral, others are more lasting. Some even become classics and contribute to imposing a new language of color.

For the manufacturer or person responsible for launching a new product, it is vital to predict the system of colors into which its products will become integrated. However, while it is difficult, indeed impossible, to predict the technical inno-

vations, it is often possible to predict the evolution of the trends and the future determinants in the world of color.

It is necessary to take into account typologies of the customer's sociocultural influences that differ from one region and country to another. "The Geography of Color" is a concept that is a concrete reality and determinant of the behavior of consumers vis-à-vis color.

The Atelier 3D Couleur method for establishing its predictions relies on the systematic analysis of the specialized international press, the study of professional expositions, and artistic expressions, just as it relies on the observations of emergences that are revealed on the street, the elaboration and the permanent updating of files of information and of syntheses. In brief, think in terms of the daily frequenting of the nebulas where trends are born and blossom (figs. 30–52).

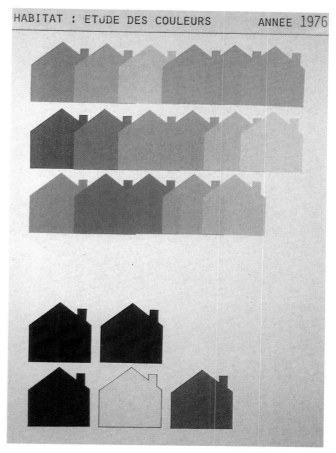

31A–31B. *1976—Plates of comparative synthesis of the dominant colors in the ready-to-wear and home industries (decoration of the home interior). From 1960 through 1965, when the colors of different components of clothing fashions began to coordinate to better harmonize and favor their assortment, colors of the fashion industry have progressively influenced the colors of the home industry. Until 1975, it could be noticed that the colors in fashion preceded the colors in homes by two years. But in 1976, as proof of these two visual syntheses, color trends of the home simultaneously rejoined those of ready-to-wear fashions. Courtesy of Atelier 3D Couleur/Jean-Philippe Lenclos.*

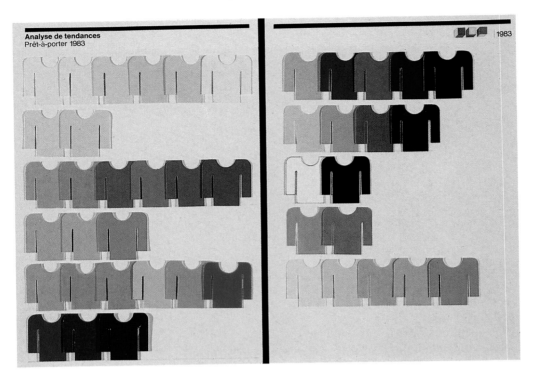

32. *1983—The synthesis of dominant colors in the ready-to-wear industry.*

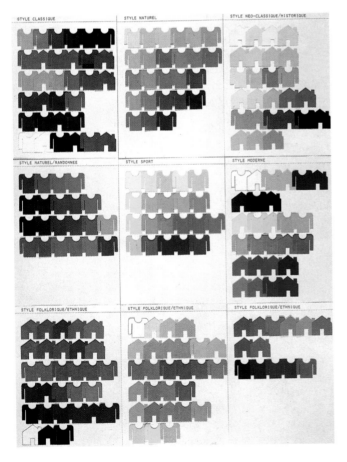

33. *1985—The methodical analysis of the evolution of colors in fashion and in the home industry have permitted Atelier 3D Couleur to release the principal trends that have appeared from 1980 on. These trends are expressed by the definition of color families which each confirm a respective dominant color. The synthesis of 1985 reveals seven principal styles of significant segments: classical style, natural style, neoclassical/historical style, natural/hiking style, sporty style, modern style, and folklore/ethnic style. These style labels have inherently evocative qualities chosen for the segment representation. They may evolve and do not constitute in any way a reference to scientific character. Courtesy of Atelier 3D Couleur/Jean-Philippe Lenclos.*

34. *Synthesis of dominant colors in the home industry in 1984. Courtesy of Atelier 3D Couleur/Jean-Philippe Lenclos.*

35A–35B. *The synthesis of dominant colors characterizing the ready-to-wear fashion industry in 1991. In this synthesis appear round illustrations showing the phenomenon of contrasts or of bi-coloring most characteristic during this period. Courtesy of Atelier 3D Couleur/Jean-Philippe Lenclos.*

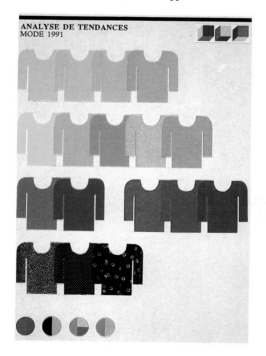
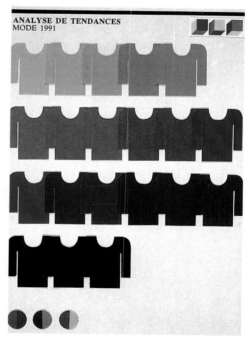

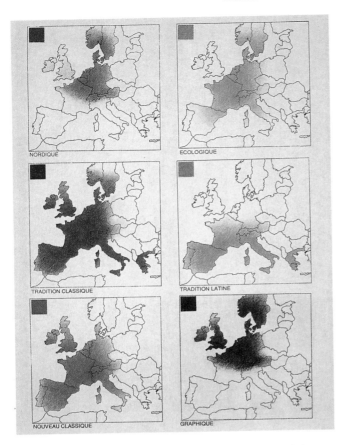

36. *Also in reference to 35B, the analytical approach of the trends in the home industry (decoration of the home interior) in European countries in 1992, confirming here the concept of "The Geography of Color" ©. In 1992, six principal trends in home colors were affirmed.*
1) Nordic—grey-tinted tonalities
2) Ecological—natural tonalities
3) Classical Tradition—dominant dark tonalities
4) Latin Tradition—warm tonalities (terra-cotta)
5) Neoclassic—wood tonalities
6) Graphic—white/black/grey
Courtesy of Atelier 3D Couleur/Jean-Philippe Lenclos.

37. *The synthesis of colors in the home industry. These illustrations symbolize the dominant colors appearing in the home in 1981 and 1984. These surroundings for the decoration and laying out of the house each relate to a typology of the specific customer picked out in the segmentation of socio-styles. In the illustration situated at the bottom right, one can observe the dominant grey and yellow confirmed in the home in 1984, but which already appeared in fashion and in automobiles in 1983. Thus, the industrial sectors, in the past distant from one another, today reveal the visual communication links where color expresses itself according to comparable schemata. Courtesy of Atelier 3D Couleur/Jean-Philippe Lenclos.*

38. *A store window in Soho, New York, in 1983. Retro fashion colors? Greys and yellows evoke the 1950s. Courtesy of Atelier 3D Couleur/Jean-Philippe Lenclos.*

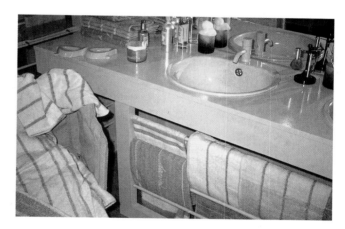

39. *Paris bathroom interior decorated in household linens from Daniel Hechter in 1984. Colors: grey and yellow. Courtesy of Atelier 3D Couleur/Jean-Philippe Lenclos.*

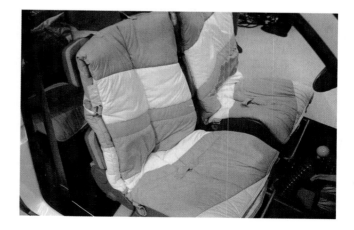

40. *Frankfurt automobile showroom in 1983. "The Junior," a small city car by Opel. Also see figure 56A for color analysis of the ready-to-wear industry in 1981 and figure 56B for color analysis of the home industry in 1981. Courtesy of Atelier 3D Couleur/Jean-Philippe Lenclos.*

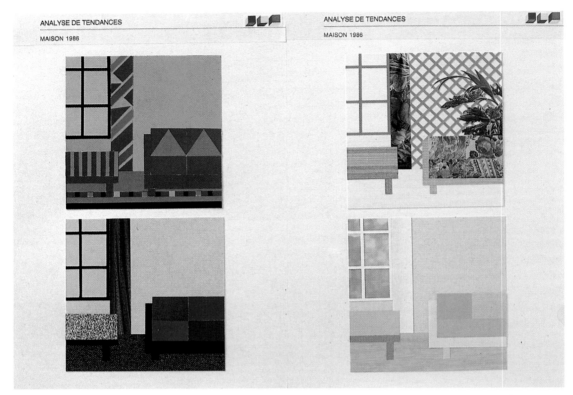

41. *Syntheses of dominant colors in the home industry emerging in 1986. Top right: greenhouse ambiance, vegetable presence. Top left, bottom right: blond and fruity tonalities. Bottom left: appearance of dominant blues Courtesy of Atelier 3D Couleur/Jean-Philippe Lenclos.*

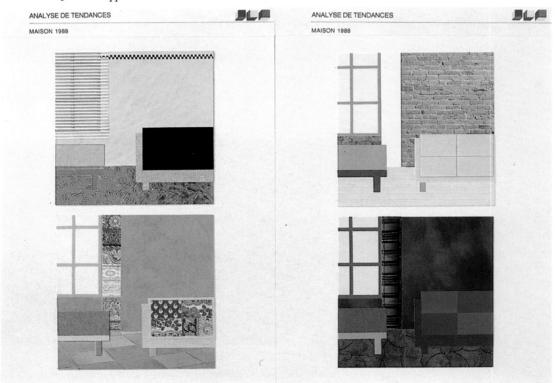

42. *Syntheses of dominant colors in the home industry emerging in 1988. Top left: technical colors and materials, metal and black Top right: soft ambiance, apparent natural materials Bottom left: traditional Mediterranean ambiance Bottom right: dark tonalities, appearance of purple Courtesy of Atelier 3D Couleur/Jean-Philippe Lenclos.*

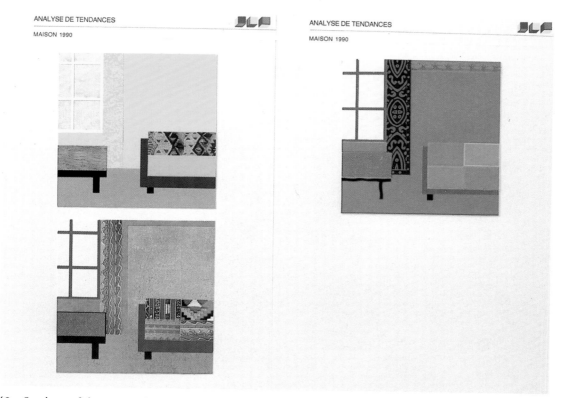

43. *Syntheses of dominant colors in the home industry emerging in 1991. Top left: influence of Van Gogh, importance of yellow Top right: flamboyant reds Bottom left: influence of the kilim tradition Courtesy of Atelier 3D Couleur/Jean-Philippe Lenclos.*

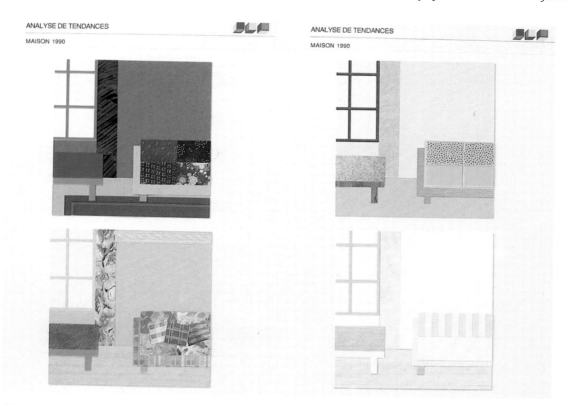

44. *Synthesis of dominant colors in the home industry emerging in 1991. Top left: the blue lets the influence of the sea appear Top right: grey-tinted pastels Bottom left: influence of the Designer Guild, English tendency to fruity tonalities Bottom right: importance of whites and colored whites Courtesy of Atelier 3D Couleur/Jean-Philippe Lenclos.*

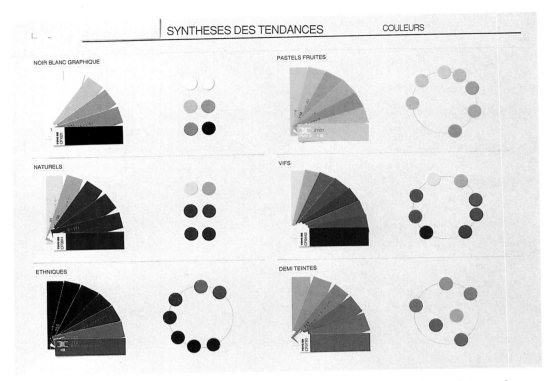

45. *Synthesis of the dominant trends appearing in the home industry in 1991. This analysis reveals the following six trends:*
    1) Graphic—black, grey, and white
    2) Naturals—sand and earth tonalities
    3) Ethnic—brown and ochre tonalities
    4) Fruity pastels—fresh and acid coloration
    5) Vivid—basic tonalities
    6) Halftones—grey-tinted tonalities
    Courtesy of Atelier 3D Couleur/Jean-Philippe Lenclos.

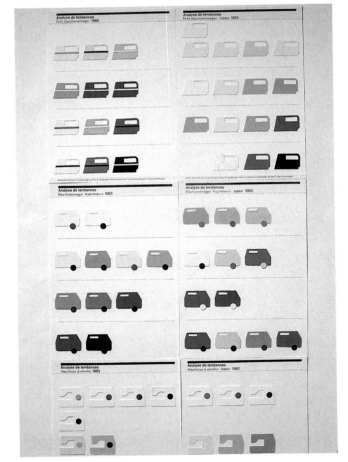

46. *Each year, Atelier 3D Couleur proceeds to analyze the trends in the household appliance industry. These synthesis plates convey the dominant account for the household appliance industry: irons, vacuum cleaners, and sewing machines. Comparison between the European market and Japan in 1984. Courtesy of Atelier 3D Couleur/Jean-Philippe Lenclos.*

47. *In 1985, Atelier 3D Couleur was asked to study the colors and decor for the range of Yamaha motorcycles destined to the European market. It was a matter of directing the motorcycle personalization by expressing each of the model typologies according to the lifestyles of their users. This plate of six collages expresses the orientations destined to the family of urban motorcycles: scooters and mopeds. At the top of the page, the two illustrations convey the "new graphic writing" able to orient the drawing of the markings or decor. The other collages convey the four trends of styles most representative in the scooter and moped category. Courtesy of Atelier 3D Couleur/Jean-Philippe Lenclos.*

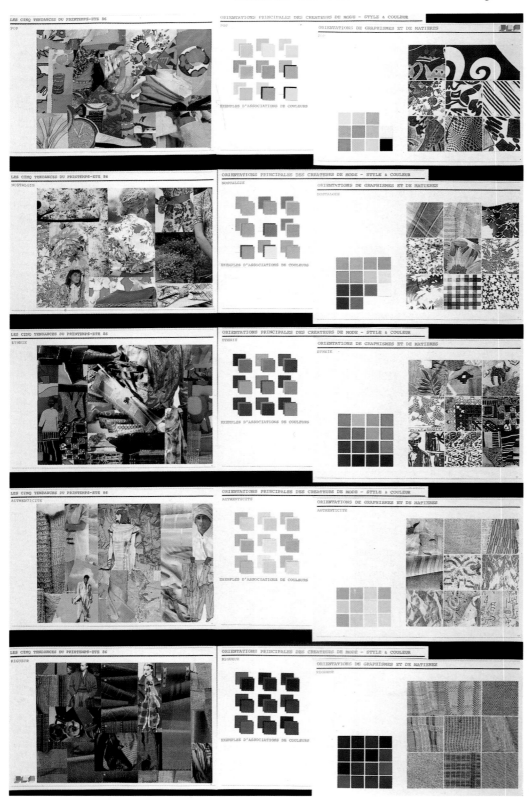

48. *Synthesis of the five dominant trends susceptible for directing the definition of a range of colors for a new pen series by Parker Pens. This prediction makes two givens appear: color and the expressions of graphics and materials.*
1) Pop   2) Nostalgia   3) Ethnic   4) Authenticity   5) Rigor
The collages illustrate the spirit and the style trend. The ranges of colors express the families and contrasts of colors. The black and white motifs express the type of decor able to serve as the graphic animation of the respective pens. Courtesy of Atelier 3D Couleur/Jean-Philippe Lenclos.

49. *Trends of colors and dominant decor in household linens in 1991. This textile industry reveals eight principal trends:*
1) Traditional Trousseau   2) Soft Geometric   3) Regionalism   4) Luminous Basics
5) Cocooning Cozy   6) Indian Company   7) New Baroque   8) Masculine Ethnic
Courtesy of Atelier 3D Couleur/Jean-Philippe Lenclos

50. *Trends of colors and dominant decor expressed in 1991 in decorative tableware. This industry is closely linked to household linens and decorative accessories. The eight dominant trends: Modern Graphic, Modern Chromatic, Decorative Symphony, Precious Ceremonial, Avant-garde Color, Baroque Chromatic, India Company, Natural Ethnic. The designation of segments voluntarily appeals to evocative words destined to illustrate each segment in a manner of imagery. Courtesy of Atelier 3D Couleur/Jean-Philippe Lenclos.*

51A. *The dominant trends expressed in 1991 in the colors for the decoration of the European home for three years, 1992/93/94. Each of the collages is accompanied by an illustration showing the synthesis of colors expressed by the collages.*
High tech house
White house
Blond house

51B. *Sante Fe house*
Yellow house
Southern house

51C. *Baroque house*
Blue house
Flowered house
Courtesy of Atelier 3D Couleur/Jean-Philippe Lenclos.

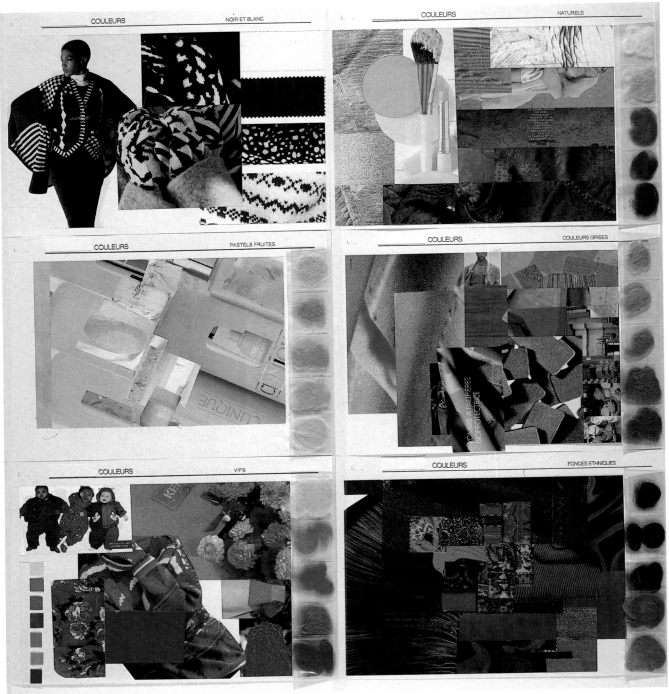

52. *Each year, the professional textile salons reveal the orientations and dominant trends for color, materials, and decor. This plate presents the synthesis of the six major trends that are revealed in the European ready-to-wear industry for the year 1992:*
   black and white
   natural
   pastel
   vibrant
   grey-tinted colors
   ethnic darks
Courtesy of Atelier 3D Couleur/Jean-Philippe Lenclos.

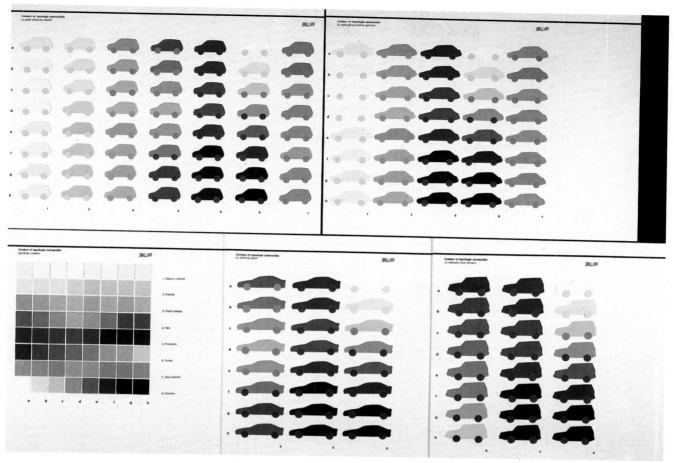

53. *The system represented on this plate was defined in 1984 for vehicles put on the market in 1988. The system proposes a range of 64 colors able to satisfy four typologies of vehicles at one manufacturer:*
  small urban model
  mid-size vehicle
  sports vehicle
  all-terrain vehicle
In 1990, '91, and '92 in auto shows in Europe, Japan, and the U.S.A., the show cars presenting certain of these pastel, fruity, grey-tinted colors reveal the exactness of this forward-looking palette. Courtesy of Atelier 3D Couleur/Jean-Philippe Lenclos.

Automobile/Transportation Industry

The automobile manufacturers always face the difficult prediction of colors for models in three or four years. The duration of this projection into the far-off future comes from the necessity in the lab to formulate body colors with the necessary time to test the good hold of pigments in the most corrosive exposure situation. The pigment quality assesses itself in about two years of exposure (figs. 53–56B).

54. *Study of trends to illustrate the interior harmonies destined to the development of Japanese automobiles. The collages, in the form of abstract compositions, convey the dominant spirit of colors that will be used in the interior of the respective automobiles. Courtesy of Atelier 3D Couleur/Jean-Philippe Lenclos.*

55. *Study of trends to illustrate the interior harmonies destined to the development of Japanese automobiles. The collages, in the form of abstract compositions, convey the dominant spirit of colors that will be used in the interior of the respective automobiles. Courtesy of Atelier 3D Couleur/Jean-Philippe Lenclos.*

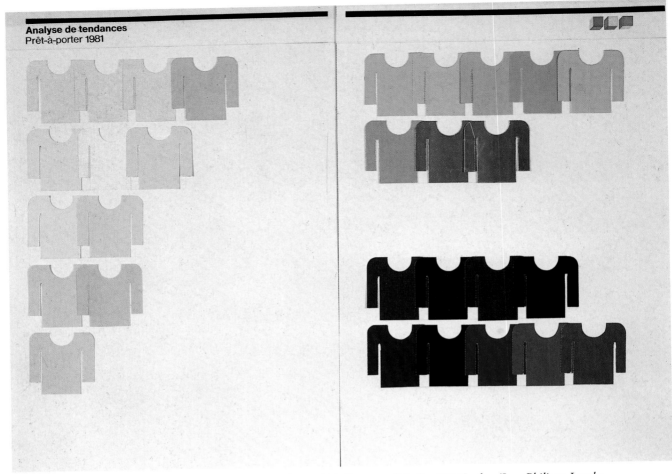

Analyse de tendances
Prêt-à-porter 1981

56A. *Ready-to-wear and home—1981. (Also refer to figure 40.) Courtesy of Atelier 3D Couleur/Jean-Philippe Lenclos.*

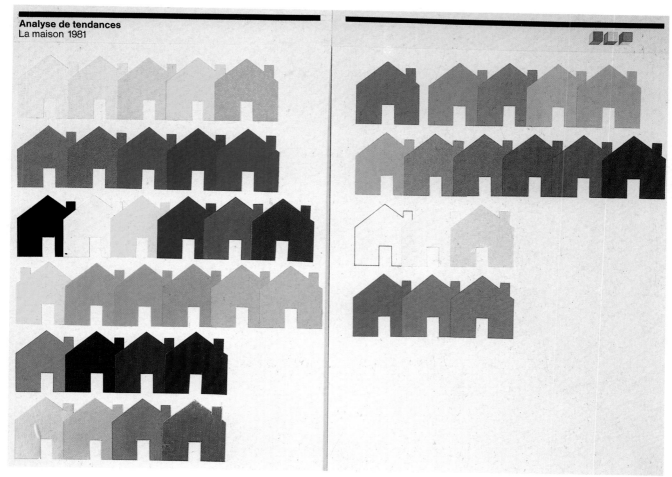

Analyse de tendances
La maison 1981

56B.

Part Two
Psychology and Color Marketing

Color directions in product design, fashion, architecture, and most other design industries have increasingly come to be recognized in the twentieth century as cyclical in nature. Tracking the cycles and trends of consumer color preferences has developed into an important support discipline and business speciality for product design and manufacturing, marketing, and sales. Marketing analysts, researchers, and psychologists make up a segment of professionals in the color forecasting field who follow and report on the dynamic indicators that are continuously affected by cultural, societal, political, and environmental circumstances.

History of the Milka Cow

Fabio Sorgesa/Jacobs Suchard

57. *Creating the Milka Cow. Courtesy of Fabio Sorgesa, Jacob Suchard AG.*

In 1972, the advertising agency Young & Rubicam came up with the idea of a cow. Today, Milka is the market leader in Germany with an annual turnover of almost DM 1 billion.

The original series of advertisements incorporated the themes of "lilac balloons," a "lilac Christmas tree," and a "lilac cow." The idea of a lilac-colored cow was borrowed from the wrapper of the Milka fullcream milk chocolate tablet. At that time, even lilac glasses were being offered in TV commercials, although half of the population was still watching black-and-white television. The play on the color lilac was finally restricted to the life-size cow only. From then on, it started whispering from billboards in Germany: "At night I'm especially tender."

An article, published in a popular daily in the past year, caused a stir when it reported that the Milka lilac was to be sent to the abattoir. Jacobs Suchard had decided to give the cow a lifetime pension.

Although the cow represents for Milka the main brand symbol of the alpine world in Germany, it has been renowned for quite some time outside of the German-speaking countries: in Italy, France, Spain, and even Argentina, in places where one would never have dreamed that the alpine scenery and the Milka cow could bear any significance (fig. 57).

Trends in Color and Pattern
Michelle Lamb

Michelle Lamb is the founder and chairperson of Marketing Directions, Inc., a company devoted to color specification and trends forecasting colors, patterns, and designs. *The Trend Curve,* published by Marketing Directions, Inc., is offered four times yearly with color and design information from major markets and trade shows that are important to the home furnishings industry (fig. 58). Below are a few questions that Ms. Lamb is often asked, adapted from her participation during the High Point Furniture market in the fall of 1992.

Q. *How long can we expect a trend to last?*

A. Typically, we see trends in color and pattern as moving along a dynamic bell curve that represents about a five-year cycle from the first time we see it until the moment it's gone. During that time, it moves from specialty retailers to department stores, then to higher volume sellers, mass merchants, and finally to low-end retailers.

When a trend is incoming, distribution is usually limited, the price is at its highest point, and retailers can expect to make their money on gross margin. As it moves along the bell curve, both the price and the margins will drop as manufacturers achieve economies of scale. However, the volume sold increases at the same time, and now the retailers rely increasingly on turnover to make their money.

What has changed over the past several years is the amount of time that it takes a trend to move beyond the high end. That cycle is speeding up somewhat. So the curve itself doesn't seem to be shortening, but it is compressing a bit in the early stages. It is, however, interesting to note that if you would divide the bell curve right down the middle, the profits are generally still equal on both sides of the curve.

Q. *What is the most important color family for the home?*

A. The role of neutrals in the home can't be underestimated. For example, in upholstery approximately 75 percent of everything that's sold is white or off white. These are considered platform for colors in many rooms. But five years ago, people were saying that this number was 80 percent.

Throughout the home, color is certainly being utilized more now than ever before. It has entered and continues to enter new categories with a high degree of acceptance.

For at least the next two years, I see a great deal of consensus surrounding greens. Green now holds the volume position that was the domain of blues just a few years ago. This doesn't mean that blues have dropped off dramatically . . . they have not. In fact, there is a hint in the air of a resurgence of blues for 1993, especially periwinkle and navy (watch especially for blue/white combinations). But greens are outselling blues from many manufacturers at this time, and will continue to do so for the next 12–18 months.

It's interesting that greens are currently most important in blue-tinted versions like teals. However, they are beginning to evolve toward more natural, yellow-tinted versions like olives, which are incoming at this time.

At the same time, browns are moving forward. For the past twelve months or so, we have seen the influence of brown creeping forward. For 1993 and 1994, the movement will be bolder, and will

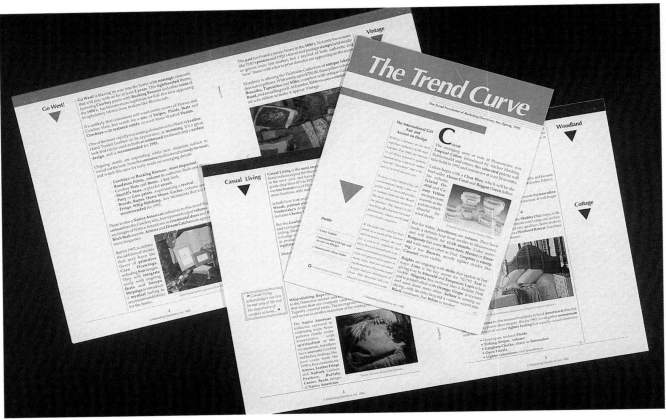

58. The Trend Curve, *a quarterly published by Marketing Directions. Photo courtesy of Michelle Lamb.*

include everything from deep chocolate browns to taupes and beiges. Think about periwinkle and taupe in combination. It's beautiful and very livable.

Q. *Are there any significant driving forces behind home trends for the 1990s?*

A. I see two major forces: nature and nostalgia.

The interest in the environment is more than a trend. It's a lifestyle change that will not fade away. In fact, it's gaining momentum. But at the same time, it is also evolving. References are becoming more subtle and more sophisticated. We're focused on integrating the details . . . an environmental motif comes together with recycled product or natural elements in a combination of earthy colors.

This movement will become stronger throughout the next several years, during which time we will stop talking about the tie-ins with Nature as though they're something new or unusual. Environmental associations will become a given.

Nostalgia is the second major force. As life

becomes more complicated, consumers are looking for patterns, styles, and color families that are friendly and familiar. They want to create environments for themselves that are safe and understandable.

This can take a variety of directions. One is playful youth, which may take us back to the cowboys on bucking broncos of our childhood; or Shabby Chic furnishings like we remember from Grandmother's house. But it can also be ethnic heritage, including arts and crafts. It can be your own or simply one that's appealing . . . a purchased history.

Q. *To what extent are trends consumer driven and to what extent industry driven? Examples of each?*

A. Industry can certainly drive trends. It happens primarily when technologies become available that allow new looks to be achieved in manufacturing (finishing vs. fibers). But for the most part, I believe that the consumer is the driving force, with industry responding.

Let's take the interest in the environment as an example. When it became clear that ecology was a topic of high interest to the consumer and would stay with us for quite some time, manufacturers immediately began responding with product that they felt would satisfy the consumer's need to represent it.

Greens became more visible. Natural materials like granite and marble became mainstream. Globe motifs and endangered animals surfaced. This fueled the consumer's interest, which, in turn, encouraged the industry to develop more products to satisfy the consumer's appetite. And as consumers have changed how they want to express their interest in the environment, the feedback has made its way back to manufacturers, who continue to look for the right way to accomplish it.

Q. *Do current events, and political, economic, or sociological concerns play a role in home furnishings style trends? If so, how?*

A. Yes, I believe that they do play a role. For example, global politics have had a dramatic effect of home furnishings. The opening up of Eastern Bloc countries in the past year or so that had previously been inaccessible to the U.S. has created an enormous interest in ethnic cultures that is now being expressed in both color combinations and in pattern.

At the same time, the economic situation in our own country has been a factor in encouraging a "less is more" philosophy of decorating that has fueled the Shaker and Mission movements. And there are many more examples.

Q. *Why has the "Lodge Look" become so successful? Has it peaked? Where will it evolve from its present form?*

A. The Lodge Look has been successful for a few key reasons:

First, it fits well with that less-is-more philosophy that sprang up after the excess of the 1980s. It appeals to basic simplicity at a time when life is certainly not simple at all. In fact, it's highly complicated to the point where a Lodge home becomes a refuge from the fast-paced world outside.

Second, Lodge also fits well with the interest in nature. Items may utilize twig looks or Native

American elements that give them a rustic feeling.

Third, this is a uniquely American look. It allows the consumer to express pride in our own heritage, and it also keys into nostalgia.

I don't believe that Lodge has peaked yet, but it is reaching down from higher-volume price points in looks that we've seen for some time, so at the high end it is evolving. I believe that the next step for it is to integrate one of two directions. The first is cowboy. This is a more lighthearted approach to the theme.

The second is "The Great Outdoors." Several manufacturers have already done a terrific job of bringing elements with a feeling of the outdoors to home furnishings. Watch for textiles prints that feature mountain scenes; the moose/elk and pine cones as motifs, primarily in giftware; and ongoing leaves, trees, plaids, buffalo checks, and sampler looks.

Q. *Is '50s Retro contrived or real, trend or passing fad?*

A. '50s Retro is just plain fun. At the same time, it's friendly and familiar to most of the consumers in this country.

If you stop for a moment to think about where the majority of consumers (the baby boom generation) are now, you might hypothesize that the largest buying public is at the point of mid-life. When that happens, there is traditionally a lot of reflection that takes place, especially in looking back into our own. The 1950s are certainly important here, as are the 1940s, both of which are a part of that generation's past. We all tend to stay within our generation.

I think that 1950s styling is a trend, and we'll see its influence in some form for a full-trend cycle of five years.

Q. *What are we seeing in terms of material other than wood . . . i.e., metals, stone, or a mixture?*

A. I believe that we have gone through the peak for interest in such stones as granite and marble. Slate is incoming but will not experience the same volume impact as the stones already mentioned. I'm seeing more emphasis on materials like glass, and in mixing materials like glass and metal for a fresh new look, as well as a mix of warm woods with metals.

Cyclic Recurrence of Collective Color Preferences

Leonhard Oberascher

Ever since the 1980s, there has been an increasing trend toward particularization of consumer demands (cf. Becker, 1991, p. 7 and Luger, 1991). In our time, self-realization and self-portrayal trends ranging from individualism to conformity determine the collective life feeling.

Nevertheless, despite this progressive particularization of consumer demands, market variety, lack of adherence to a certain style, and general design preferences can be observed. This is especially obvious in the use of color.

Since 1987 there has been a continuous rise in the proportion of purple colors or color combinations with purple (especially in Germany, Austria, and Switzerland). It is remarkable that this trend was not confined to certain types of products but encompassed every imaginable field. For instance, in the case of new buildings or conversions, architects increasingly resorted to the use of purple tones, although they have usually been against the use of "in" colors. Advertising also made increasing use of these colors, including complete surface areas printed in full chromatic color, which appear to have no direct relationship to the message of the advertisement. The color itself became the message. Purple had always been regarded negatively in literature on color psychology (tension, reluctance, disquiet, renunciation, etc.) but it underwent a positive change in significance. It became a new trend color, and in combination with turquoise (figs. 59A–D) often signified modernity, fashion, and trend awareness.

Although other colors (e.g., achromatic, black, and highly chromatic colors) were found on the

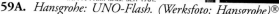

59A. *Hansgrohe: UNO-Flash. (Werksfoto: Hansgrohe)®*

59B. *Photo courtesy of Leonhard Oberascher.*

59D. *Photo courtesy of Leonhard Oberascher.*

59C. *Helmut Taube GmbH: Kinderzimmer Melina.*

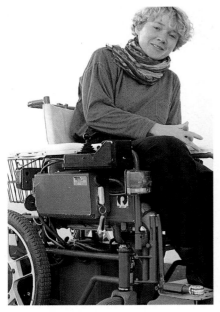

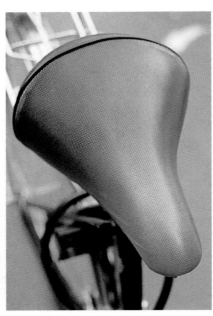

60A. *Photo courtesy of Leonhard Oberascher.*

60B. *Photo courtesy of Leonhard Oberascher.*

60C. *Franz Wittmann Mobelwerkstatten: Modell SANTOS.*

60D. *Photo courtesy of Leonhard Oberascher.*

60E. *Photo courtesy of Leonhard Oberascher.*

60F. *Photo courtesy of Leonhard Oberascher.*

market between 1987 and 1992, since 1989 a "collective trend" (i.e., general color preference in all target groups for purple or color combinations containing purple), became evident and purple became the dominant color of these years (figs. 60A–F).

However, the overwhelming success of purple color nuances was not unexpected. A survey of color trends over the last twenty years shows this phenomenon to result from a systematic development.

Color Cycles

"The kind of predominant style has been periodically transformed in Western civilization. In each case the system of order developed from the simple to the complex, in order to return to simplicity following saturation."[1] This is how J. K. Grutter describes the change in style of Western architecture (Grutter, 1987, p. 37). Color assignment—as a component of the visual system of order in architecture—is subject to a similar change.

Werner Spillmann shows in his article published in 1981, "Architektur zwischen Grau und Superbunt" that color assignment in Western architecture swings between the two extremes of chromatic and achromatic. Christel Darmstadt, who studied the historic color concepts of buildings (1982, 1985, and 1987), made the observation that color changes take place regularly and recur cyclically. She demonstrated that between 1860 and the present, four marked color cycles have occurred, in which each case had similar characteristics and lasted between fifteen and twenty-five years.

The beginning of each cycle is dominated by highly chromatic colors and multicoloredness, later replaced by less chromatic (subdued) colors. The earth colors (brown tones) became popular and were finally replaced by achromatic colors (white, grey, and black). This phase was again replaced by highly chromatic colors and, thus, a new cycle began.

Independently of this, Udo Koppelmann and Erich Kuthe from the University of Cologne (1987, pp. 113–22) determined a similar color sequence in a study they did on the acceptance of colors used for sanitary purposes.

New Empirical Studies

Koppelmann and Kuthe based their study on an analysis of the color design of the cover page of *Schöner Wohnen* (Beautiful Living), a German magazine on interior design, published from 1970 to 1985. The central idea of their approach was that color trends for the living area are sensitively monitored by the major commercial journals on interior design and are reflected visually in the title page design.

As we considered this study to be particularly suitable for a critical investigation of the color-cycle thesis, we have made it the basis of a new study, extending the time span and expanding the content. However, as we considered an evaluation of the color design of the cover pages—as carried out by Koppelmann and Kuthe—to be insufficient for a differentiated analysis of the periodic sequence of dominant colors used in home furnishings, we perused the journals from 1972 to 1992 many times, paying particular attention to trend subjects, furnishing suggestions, and advertisements for living-room and kitchen furniture. Using the Natural Color System (NCS), we estimated the dominant colors of individual illustrations, evaluated them according to their occurrence frequency, and selected the most typical colors from the NCS collection of color samples. We were, thus, able to document the former trend colors relatively precisely and reconstruct their periodic sequence (cf. Oberascher, 1991) and also show the principles of color design for each individual phase.

The following waves of color preference in the living area between 1972 and 1992 are shown in simplified form from our analysis:

1972 highly chromatic colors, multicoloredness

from 1974 darker colors

from 1976 earth colors, especially brown tones

from 1979 lighter colors, light, natural colors, beige, off white

from 1981 trend toward pure white

from 1984 achromatic colors (pure white, grey, anthracite, black)

from 1988 chromatic colors in combination with highly chromatic colors

from 1991 shades of purple and an increase in highly chromatic colors

To make results of our study clearer, we have selected more than 200 illustrations from *Schöner Wohnen* but can only show a few typical examples here (figs. 61–69).

---

1. Translation by the author.

61. *Gruner + Jahr:* Schöner Wohnen, *Vol. 3, 1972. Photograph: Willig.*

62. *Gruner + Jahr:* Schöner Wohnen, *Vol. 10, 1976. Photograph: Vollborn.*

63. *Gruner + Jahr:* Schöner Wohnen, *Vol. 8, 1977. Photograph: Rogers.*

64. *Gruner + Jahr:* Schöner Wohnen, *Vol. 5, 1979. Photograph: Stradtmann.*

65. *Gruner + Jahr:* Schöner Wohnen, *Vol. 4, 1980. Photograph: Willig.*

66. *Gruner + Jahr:* Schöner Wohnen, *Vol. 9, 1985. Photograph: Norenberg/Heide.*

67. *Gruner + Jahr:* Schöner Wohnen, *Vol. 7, 1987. Photograph: Schmutz.*

68. *Gruner + Jahr:* Schöner Wohnen, *Vol. 11, 1991. Photograph: Stradtmann.*

69. *Gruner + Jahr:* Schöner Wohnen, *Vol. 11, 1991.*
Photograph: Stradtmann.

The results of our study present additional and more precise information about the picture analysis carried out by Koppelmann and Kuthe and confirm the principal supposition of a cyclical recurrence of collective color preferences or color trends: highly chromatic colors (chromatic phase) signify the start of a new color cycle; this phase is replaced by one of darker colors (darkening phase), followed by a gradual transition to autumnal color nuances (brown phase). These colors then become lighter, tending toward beige/off white and are complemented by pastel colors (lighter phase). The lighter colors become paler and paler, and then white and shades of grey are dominant (achromatic phase). After a while the achromatic colors are combined with highly chromatic colors (achromatic-chromatic phase) and purple nuances (purple phase) become widespread. Finally, the achromatic colors disappear almost completely and highly chromatic colors again come to the fore.

The success of purple nuances described earlier corresponds well with expected color preference in accordance with the assumed cyclical recurrence of color trends. Koppelmann remarked that purple adopts an intermediary role between achromatic and chromatic phases and, thus, indicates an imminent new color cycle. The increase in highly chromatic color suggests that in 1992 and 1993 (at least in the German-speaking area) we are indeed at the beginning of a new color cycle. People have become tired of looking at the "cool," stylized "high-tech-line."[2] Rounded, soft, organic forms are again in demand. "Loud" colors and intense contrasts of color are considered refreshing. Young people discover pop art. As in the 1960s, highly chromatic colors offer a possibility of

2. The change from one color phase to another can be explained on the basis of dynamism of need, according to appropriate visual stimulation (avoidance of too little stimulation or overstimulation) and the evolution theory (cf. Schuster, 1985, pp. 36, 41, 377; Koppelmann and Kuthe, 1987, pp. 121–22).

General Principles of Color Design

On the basis of a detailed analysis of the color combinations typical for each wave of color preference in furnishing examples published between 1972 and 1992, we were able to deduce the following general color design rules for the individual color phases (fig. 70).

Chromatic phase

Distinctively polychrome (multicolored) and intense contrasts of hue (opposing and contrasting hues; e.g., orange-green) are characteristic of the phase.

Darkening phase

The polychrome aspect remains but the contrasting hues become less intense and are darker. The common characteristic of the colors is the same or there is a similar perceived resemblance with black (similar blackness, veiled black, black association).

Brown phase

The darkened color range is limited to a few hues (ranging between yellow and red). Colors are characterized by a similarity in hue (matching tones).

Lighter phase

The range of brown colors becomes lighter and tends toward beige and off white. It is complemented by pastel colors. The range of color again becomes more varied but the colors are determined by the same or a similar perceived resemblance with white (similar whiteness, veiled white, white association) and similarly by related nuances (similar value).

Achromatic phase

Colors become paler and paler. Neutral white is dominant and is increasingly complemented by light grey, then medium grey, dark grey, anthracite, and black. Colors are achromatic or weakly chromatic (greyish nuances). Design is largely limited to contrasts of lightness.

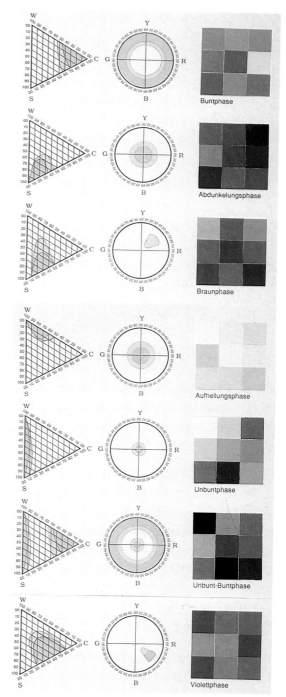

70. *Photo courtesy of Leonhard Oberascher.*

Achromatic–Chromatic phase

Achromatic colors are combined with highly chromatic (or sometimes medium chromatic) colors. A variety of subtle color combinations is thereby possible. The dominant principle of design is the contrast of chroma (achromatic and more or less chromatic colors are contrasted with one another).

Purple phase

The color range is limited to a very small segment of the hue circle (between NCS R30B and R60B). Purple can stand on its own or be combined with other colors. Both matching tone combinations (reddish purple and bluish purple) and contrasting combinations (purple and turquoise) are possible.

Summary and Discussion

The rapid periodic change in style from simplicity to complexity in Western civilization can be traced back a long way. With change, predominant colors for a period are also changed.

As the range of available colors is by its nature limited,[3] a repetition of color design measures becomes obvious. Various studies mentioned in this article have demonstrated a cyclical sequence of preferred colors used in architectural and interior design. There is also empirical evidence that the same concept applies to other design qualities, such as product shape and outline (Abshof, 1991).

A model of cyclic recurrence of color preference, therefore, seems to be plausible. As in all probability, a cyclic recurrence of color trends follows the pattern described in this article, this can form the basis for long-term forecasts of color preference that can be useful in designing new products.

However, the "fine-tuning" of trend colors or selections of new color combinations is not predicted by this model. For this and the following reasons, selecting the "right" colors for the future will remain a crucial task for designers, color consultants, and marketing experts.

An important limitation in the forecast of collective color preferences is that although people may belong to the same cultural group, not everyone is prepared to go along with collective color changes. In the study *Wohnwelten in Deutschland II* (Concepts of Living in Germany II), published in 1988, the authors Becker and Flaig present nine taste dimensions for living, and in each case they trace the preference back to the various range of values and life attitudes of different groups of people (or social milieus).[4] Various color preferences can probably be deduced from knowledge about differences in range of values and attitudes to life of different social milieus.

It is to be expected that people with traditional attitudes adhere more to a "traditional color world" than those with more liberal and unconventional attitudes. The maintenance of a traditional life order also demands the maintenance of its traditional symbols. The colors or color combinations typical of traditional color conventions, thus, form a component part of the visual reference system of social classes with traditional attitudes.

Therefore, willingness to adopt new ideas seems to be a prerequisite for the acceptance of a new color range. However, no systematic study has yet been made as to whether and to what extent color preferences of various groups are influenced by new color trends.

Another reason for why selecting the "right" colors will remain a crucial task is that even if it is likely that a group of people will adopt new color trends, a cyclic recurrence of color preference does not imply that colors are reinterpreted and used the same way that they were interpreted and used

---

3. The development of new pigments, dyeing processes, and surface techniques does, indeed, offer the designer new creative possibilities within a limited framework; however, new colors cannot in principle be discovered. The number of possible colors is predetermined by human perception of color. Although a person with normal color perception is able to differentiate about 10 million color nuances (cf. Judd and Wyszecki, 1975), he classifies these in a few typical groups of color (cf. Oberascher, 1989).

---

4. The term *social milieu* (translation of the German original "Soziales Milieu") was adopted by Becker and Flaig to describe a group of people with a similar view and way of life, similar personal attitudes, motives and dispositions, wishes, and expectations from life.

before. In particular, young people tend to interpret them on the basis of their present values, norms, and attitudes. They will use "old" colors in a new context and fit them into their individual lifestyle scenery. In this respect, the mass media may contribute to the consolidation of new trends by "smoothing" different tendencies and integrating them into a uniform "picture," with which the consumer can easily identify (cf. Hebdinge, 1983; Luger, 1991).

Finally, other factors, such as technical and ergonomic reasons, psychological and metaphysical concepts, color harmony and personal color styling (e.g., "Color Me Beautiful") may restrict the influence of color trends on the consumers' final color choice.

However, as this article shows, a well-founded investigation of color design trends offers valuable insights that can be used specifically to increase market advantages by trend-adjusted color design. In addition to a further empirical study of the color preference model described here, further studies will be necessary on the correlation between general target-group color trends and group-specific (or milieu-specific) color preferences, in order to develop a differentiated instrument for ascertaining and forecasting collective color preferences for trade and industry.

Bibliography

Abshof, I. A. *Modeprognosen.* Proceedings of Wirus-Designer-Runde 1991. Pfleiderer Industrie: Neumarkt, 1991.

Becker, U., "Die Trendsetter auf dem Weg ins Zeitgeistmuseum?" in *Dokumentation Wirus-Designer-Runde*, 23–24 May 1991, pp. 36–116.

———— and B. Flaig. *Wohnwelten in Deutschland II,* 2nd edition. Burda und Sinus: 1989.

Darmstadt, C. "Farbige Fassungen für Bürgerhauser des Historismus und des Jugendstils unter heutigen Aspekten." Dissertation, Dortmund University, 1982.

———— "Farbe in der Architektur ab 1800," in *DBZ,* 6 Juni 1987, pp. 743–48.

———— "Farbenbewegungen in der Architektur-gestaltung." Unpublished manuscript. Bottrop: 1985.

Grutter, J. K. *Asthetik der Architektur.* Stuttgart: Kohlhammer, 1987.

Hebdinge, D. "Subculture, die Bedeutung von Stil" in *Schocker, Stile und Moden der Subkultur,* ed. D. Diederichsen, D. Hebdinge, O. D. Marx. Reinbeck bei Hamburg: Rowohlt Taschenbuch Verlag GmbH, 1983, pp. 8–114.

Judd, D. B., and Wyszecki, G.: *Colour in Business, Science and Industry,* 3rd edition. New York: Wiley, 1975.

Koppelmann, U. "Verkaufsentscheidend: die richtige Farbe zur richtigen Zeit" in *Methodik III,* 1989, pp. 166–68.

———— and Kuthe, E. "Präferenzwellen beim Gestaltungsmittel Farbe" in *Marketing-ZFP,* Vol. 2, 1987, pp. 113–22.

Luger, K. "Freizeitmuster und Lebensstil/Medien als Kompositeure, Segmenteure und Kolporteure." Unpublished manuscript. Salzburg University: 1991.

NCS. *Natural Colour Systems, Colour Atlas,* 2nd ed. Stockholm: SIS, 1989.

Oberascher, L. "Memory for Colors: Evidence for a universal color language?" in *AIC—COLOR 89,* Vol. 2, Buenos Aires, Argentina. Proceedings of the 6th Session of the Association Internationale de la Coleur. San Martín (BA): Grupo Argentino del Color, 1989.

———— "Colour in marketing: Is there any reliability in the anticipation of the colours to come?" in Introduction to the Proceedings of AIC-Conference "Colour and Light," Sidney, 1991.

Riedel, I. *Farben,* 7th edition. Stuttgart: Kreuz Verlag, 1989.

Schuster, M. *Das ästhetische Motiv.* Frankfurt/Main: Fachbuchhandlung für psychologie GmbH, Verlagsabteilung, 1985.

Schöner Wohnen, Vols. 1972–92. Hamburg: Gruner +Jahr AG & Co. Druck- und Verlaghaus.

Spillmann, W. "Architektur zwischen Grau und Superbunt" in *Aktuelles Bauen,* Vol. 4, 1981.

Display Design/Design Etc., Inc.

Don Campbell

A decade of exemplary service and unique design has placed Design Etc., Inc. (DEI) among the leading design firms in the world. By combining a design studio with a visual merchandising department, and by adding a variety of related skills (lighting, scenic techniques, etc.), we provide comprehensive design and display services to a wide range of markets.

Founded more than ten years ago as a full-service design and display company, DEI has proven that its design philosophy was well grounded. In the last decade, DEI has grown and expanded by over 60 percent each year, in 1992 designing and project-managing exhibits in six countries with budgets of over 5.5 million dollars. Looking forward, DEI hopes to take its present size and varied skills and refine them into one of the most skilled and successful commercial/exhibition design firms in the field.

"Listen to what the client says." Often said, but seldom done. DEI spends quite some time sifting through marketing rhetoric and proffered solutions to distill the basic requirements. "Seek to present each client in a specific and unique manner." In much commercial design, the designers simply fall back on accepted conventions or the latest trends and miss the imperative of setting the client apart from the competitors. (In any exhibition hall, try this trick: Rearrange the logos on the stands. Does it make a difference?) Remember why we're all here. Generally speaking, it's to sell a product or service. That is the only reason for having an exhibit. It's not to promote the latest design; it's not to sell your design. DEI has developed a complete department staff to control and edit the designs, so as to comply with the display of products. We also attend the installation and visually merchandise the product.

DEI has developed a reputation for dedication to all budgets: time, materials, and money. Adding total project management in developing budgets, acting as owner's representative with shops and contractors, managing products, hiring and managing show staff, etc., have evolved into a full-service offering. Recently, DEI has added another innovative offering to the package. We discovered that creating quality props, scenic painting, and other specialized techniques often perplex conventional shops, but has enabled us to bring together a fine department of crafts encompassing all of these techniques (figs. 71–78).

71. *"Milton Bradley/Playskool France": Exhibition Stand for Toyfair, Paris 1990. The brief's primary plank consisted of a request to establish a graphic image that would be unique and easily retained by the buyers as distinctly theirs. The competitor's facades (as well as MB's) had been mostly white and very traditional corporate colors (standard exhibition: dark blue, dark red, etc.). We decided first on using a color palette that would be innovative and playful as an expression of the current marketing trends (an exhibition stand is, after all, a temporary structure and can and often should echo "trendy" design vocabularies without dating itself). Second, we sought two divergent elements that would each express the personality of the two companies and yet live in harmony. This led to the use of the over-scale building blocks (Playskool's preschool and baby product) and the black-and-white checkerboard (echoing MB's position as a world leader in games). The success of this design can be measured not only in accolades from the design industry (several European design awards and inclusion in several books and publications) but also in the fact that now most of the stands at this fair have "brushed up" their facades and no longer look like carbon copies of each other. Photograph courtesy of Don Campbell and P & G Photographers, Paris.*

72. "Baby Wanna Walk" (Hasbro Showroom, U.S.A.): an interesting design problem in creating a contemporary feeling while echoing the traditional values and play patterns of the product. This doll in particular was interesting because it was a truly innovative product (first independently crawling and then walking doll ever developed) and yet reflective of very traditional dolls. We decided that we'd use a color range and palette that would be reminiscent of those colors and patterns from most of the buyers' childhoods. The colors are based on nursery and playroom palettes from the late 1940s and 1950s. The wall murals reflect the popular "cartoon" looks of children's books of the era. To add a sense of domestic life, comfortable furnishings were selected and included in the scene with careful attention given to painted details. It is often possible to add a feeling of "home" to an exhibit by introducing a window that has "sunlight" streaming in and, in doing so, you'll achieve two important marks: first, the warm feeling of being protected, and second, a sense of place in being somewhere other than in the middle of a commercial building. Photo courtesy of Bo Parker.

73A. *"G.I. Joe" (Hasbro Showroom, U.S.A.): Although G.I. Joe is essentially a military concept, it has become over the years more of a part of our youth culture (without passing judgment as to being good or bad). The client requested that we do something different here and design a space that would reflect several important points: 1) confidence and presence in the marketplace as one of the most successful products ever; 2) innovation of product and not taking this leadership position for granted; 3) reinforcement of the cartoon aspect of play as a reminder of how the play pattern works and the removal of the product from the reality of the military. Since Joe has one of the most successful comic books in the industry, we used this as a springboard for achieving all of the above. Using galvanized metals for the walls, we created a neutral base that would be interesting and not compete with the "art." We added bright polished chrome edging to the metal wall panels to catch the color and light from the neon detailing on the cartoon panels. The bright, colorful nature of the "art" also meant that it would be interesting to continue this neutral approach to all furnishings, letting the "art" be set rather jewel-like into the setting. Splashes of color were also introduced within the lighting. So here we have a design that is quite colorful and bright which in reality is completely based on using just one overall color (silver) in a variety of textures. In controlling the amount of color we were able to ensure our messages would be seen and thus heard. Photo courtesy of Bo Parker.*

74. *"New Kids on the Block" (fashion dolls, Hasbro Showroom, U.S.A.): hot, trendy merchandising at its most intensive. This is a relatively simple design using icon elements from the fashion and music worlds that shout "NOW." Glazed-brick walls with graffiti and neon. Above there is a lighting truss hung heavy with theatrical lights and panning spots. On the opposite wall is a bank of video monitors all showing different images from concerts and interviews. Magazine articles and headlines about Kids are blown up and pasted to these walls as well. The floor is hard (as opposed to the carpeting used elsewhere). All of this activity and chaos is important in setting the mood; however, it is important to retain focus on the product being presented (sold). To do this, we used a black tube metal grid attached to the walls. This brought an order and organization to the space and also acted as a division between the activity and visual noise on one side and the calm required for proper presentation on the other. Photo courtesy of Bo Parker.*

75. *"Tongue-Ties" (Hasbro Showroom, U.S.A.): Often the most brief and simple products bring about the most successful exhibits. This stand-alone exhibit works especially well. We did not know where it would end up in the showroom and had been told that it would be used elsewhere after the show. We decided that some sort of kiosk would suit the bill. Since it needed to explain the entire toy concept and show the product line (over 20 different variations), it was treated with a visual humor. The large sneaker with large tongue-tie lips does both. The group of folks crammed into the two side units (doing what we'll never know) invites a smile and shows our product in real scale in use. The laces up each side show the entire line and the space inside provided for storage of samples. The bright colors are guaranteed to attract and hold attention no matter where the unit is placed. Photo courtesy of Bo Parker.*

76. *"Survivor Shot" (Hasbro Showroom, New York City): This unusual design features only black light as the light source. The room for this product display was very narrow and not too deep (11 feet by 16 feet). The product is a laser tag game meant to be played outdoors. We decided that an urban setting would be interesting and we wanted to make a display that would remove the gun aspect and replace it with the high-tech. To widen the space and fool the eye into seeing a larger presentation than we actually had, the cityscape was constructed from concrete reinforcement bars in forced perspective painted with fluorescent paint. Behind this was a grey mosaic mirrored wall that fragmented and multiplied the image (further pushing the walls back). Added to the composition were various targets encouraging visitors to try their hand. Photo courtesy of Bo Parker.*

77. *"Monster Face" (Hasbro Showroom, New York City): a dark, dank and mysterious space for a little creative play in rearranging the natural order of things like noses and ears! By keeping the surrounding walls and details in neutral colors and then adding a warmer and unique color center (the rustic brown worktable) we not only added atmosphere but kept focus on the product and packaging. Photo courtesy of Barry Pribula.*

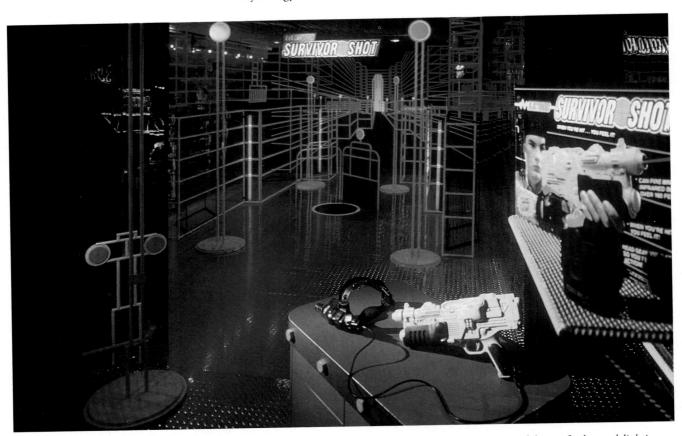

78. *"Playskool Lobby" (New York City Showroom): Although the walls are flat and not very deep, careful use of color and lighting add depth and detail. A handsome and simple solution that leads the eye inward. Photo courtesy of Barry Pribula. Lighting by Ken Farley.*

Fashions in House Paint

The Efforts of the Paint Industry to Influence Popular Color Taste for American Domestic Architecture Exteriors at the Turn of the Twentieth Century

Christine B. Hilke

In recent years, experts in the fields of architectural history and paint analysis have become increasingly interested in the identification and reproduction of historic paint colors. This trend reflects the advances in chemical and microscopic technology that have made accurate reproduction of historic colors possible. Use of these techniques at sites such as Mount Vernon and Monticello has added to our ability to interpret more accurately historic architecture. While the literature has identified the colors that enjoyed popularity in the past, studies investigating the factors that influenced the choice of specific exterior paint colors have been conspicuously absent.[1] This essay will explore the history of early-twentieth-century color forecasting and tastemaking, with regard to American domestic architecture exteriors. Particular emphasis will be placed on an advertising campaign conducted in 1907 and 1908 which profoundly altered the marketing approaches of paint manufacturers to the homeowners.

Examination of manuals for painters, architectural guidebooks, brochures issued by paint manufacturers, and trade and popular journals since the mid-nineteenth century, as well as histories of the paint industry, reveals a decided shift over the years in the methods employed to influence popular taste in colors.[2] During a seventy-five-year period of growth and industrialization in the United States, the specific groups and individuals who played the role of tastemaker changed. While the factors that precipitated this remain unexplored, the end result is clear. By 1920, the color tastes of American homeowners were guided by sophisticated publications and calculated forecasts issued by major business concerns and forecasting committees. Because of these publications, paint as a commodity shifted in the minds of the public from a product used to protect and maintain a structure to one that enhanced and beautified it.

Throughout most of the nineteenth century, the individuals who advocated specific color choices for exterior decoration were primarily promoting their own tastes. These self-proclaimed forecasters or color experts included architectural critics and builders such as Andrew Jackson Downing, Calvert Vaux, and Marriott Field, as well as local master painters.[3] In addition, the writers and editors of such popular periodicals as the *Ladies' Home Journal* (edited by Edward Bok), with its column

---

1. An example of the excellent reviews of early-twentieth-century color palettes among the literature is Roger Moss, *Century of Color: Exterior Decoration for American Buildings—1820/1920* (Watkins Glen, New York: American Life Foundation, 1981).

2. Resources are diverse. Among these are two comprehensive histories of the paint industry: George B. Heckel, *The Paint Industry: Reminiscences and Comments* (St. Louis: American Paint Journal Company, 1928) and Ernest T. Trigg, *Fifty-Five Colorful Years* (Stonington, Conn.: The Pequot Press, 1954). A sampling of early publications issued by manufacturers includes: John W. Masury, *Plain Talk with Practical Painters* (New York: John Masury & Son, 1872); *How Every Man Can Paint and Select Colors* (Ingersoll Paint Works, 1873); *House Painting* (Cleveland: The Sherwin-Williams Company, 1883); and *What Color?* (Cleveland: The Sherwin-Williams Company, 1885). Trade and popular journals include: *American Paint and Oil Dealer; Collier's Magazine; Drugs, Oils and Paints; House Painting and Decorating; Ladies' Home Journal;* and *Oil Paint and Drug Reporter.* Among prominent in-house publications issued for plant employees and salesmen are: *The Chameleon, The Colorist,* and *The S.W.P.,* all issued by the Sherwin-Williams Company; and *The Dutch Boy Painter,* published by the National Lead Company.

3. See works such as Andrew Jackson Downing, *Country Residences* (New York: Wiley & Putnam, 1842); Andrew Jackson Downing, *The Architecture of Country Homes* (New York: D. Appleton & Co., 1850); Marriott Field, *Rural Architecture* (New York: Miller, 1857); Calvert Vaux, *Villas and Cottages* (New York: 1857); and E.K. Rossiter and F.A. Wright, *Modern House Painting* (New York: 1882). Other sources include painters' manuals, such as Charles L. Condit, *Painting and Painters' Materials: A Book of Facts for Painters and Those Who Use or Deal in Paint Materials* (The Railroad Gazette, 1883); O.A. Roorbach, *The Painter's Handbook* (New York, 1868); and Henry C. Baird, *The Painter, Guilder, and Varnisher's Companion,* Vol. 1., (Philadelphia: T.K. and P.G. Collins, 1850).

"Good Taste, Bad Taste," worked to influence public views on the matter. Other than these limited resources, middle-class American homeowners had few guides for painting their houses. By the end of the century, however, this situation began to change. The role of tastemaker shifted from individuals to paint manufacturers and their trade associations. As these groups sought to increase paint sales and control consumption habits, they moved into the role of primary influencer of color taste for American homeowners.

During the last quarter of the nineteenth century, preliminary attempts by the paint manufacturers to influence taste were twofold. First, they published for the homeowner books and pamphlets that emphasized harmonious color schemes. Second, in-house journals and periodicals were made available to paint dealers, salesmen, and employees of the manufacturing concerns. While a few large and expensive books, such as those issued by Devoe or Lucas, stood out among the early literature, most publications were of a far more primitive nature.[4] The paint companies, which had previously issued relatively basic color cards, began to expand on this means of promotion. By 1900, many of these cards identified colors by name, as well as by number. The last two decades of the nineteenth century witnessed rapid expansion for these manufacturers. Their growth and increased promotional activities were a direct result of the rapid rise in population in the country, which resulted in higher demand and thus escalated competition. These changes were also related to advances in transportation and printing techniques.[5] The related surge of printed material reflected the increasing sophistication of the paint industry and represented the first instance in which middle-class homeowners had access to professionally presented information.

With regard to these early activities is an experimental advertising campaign conducted in 1907 and 1908. The brainchild of members of the Bureau of Promotion and Development of the Paint Manufacturers' Association of the United States, the campaign's objective was to create fashion trends within the house painting industry and to convince homeowners of the importance of these trends. While the clear intent of the campaign was to increase paint sales and limit the number of colors that needed to be manufactured (in other words, limit variety), it appeared to have a significant impact on the entire industry's promotional strategies.

The campaign was originally the idea of Tom Neal, director of the professional section of the Bureau of Promotion and Development, and a founder of the Acme White Lead and Color Works. At the time of the proposal, manufacturers found themselves required to produce an ever-expanding number of shades and tints in an effort to compete with one another. Neal's suggestion was presented as a possible solution to this problem. By limiting the variety of colors produced, manufacturers could decrease the demands of production and focus on establishing a desire for a higher-grade and more expensive product. Neal argued that there should be a controlled list of colors dictated by fashion. He believed that the methods employed by the manufacturers of women's apparel—whereby the leading dressmakers agreed among themselves on which colors to produce—could be adapted to work in the paint industry.[6] The 1907–1908 dates of the campaign were significant, as formal forecasting for the women's garment industry in the United States did not take place until 1915.[7] The committee agreed that the concept was feasible and began working out the campaign to promote fashionable paint colors.

---

4. F.W. Devoe and Company, *Exterior Decoration. A treatise on the artistic use of colors in the ornamentation of buildings, and a series of designs, illustrating the effects of different combinations of colors in connection with various styles of architecture* (New York, 1885), reprinted by The Athenaeum of Philadelphia, 1976; *Modern House Painting Designs* (Philadelphia: Lucas Paint Works, 1887).

5. See Moss, *Century of Color,* pp. 10–11.

6. George B. Heckel, *The Paint Industry: Reminiscences and Comments* (St. Louis: American Paint Journal Company, 1928), p. 393.

7. Unpublished records (meeting minutes, 1914–1915) of the Color Association of the United States. Located at the Hagley Museum and Library, Wilmington, Del., Manuscripts Division.

Preliminary planning began with the selection of two hues: a shade of brown and a shade of green. The committee chose these colors because they had learned that they were to be featured in dress goods for women for the upcoming season. To add interest to the campaign, George Heckel, editor and publisher of the trade journal *Drugs, Oils and Paints,* and secretary of the Paint Manufacturers' Association, named the hues "copper brown" and "copper verde."[8] The bureau then sent out one-pound samples of the paints to all members of the Association. Many manufacturers agreed to make the colors.[9]

The committee then began to convince master painters and architects of the validity of the idea. The Bureau presented a series of lectures to the Michigan Chapter of the American Institute of Architects at their regular monthly meeting on June 4, 1907. In a speech entitled "Fashions in House Paint," Heckel presented the new campaign to the architects. His talk began with a discussion of fashion in general. He commented that "changing fashions are one of the indications of progress, while unchanging convention marks a people at a stand-still or in decadence. Progressive peoples invent and originate; unprogressive peoples imitate and inherit."[10] In a comparison to music and the arts, he elaborated,

It is a far cry from Michaelangelo and Richard Wagner to humble house painting; yet, in one phase, house paint is an element of the beauty with which civilized man seeks to surround himself, and it is subject to the same fundamental laws which govern the fit and the unfit, the beautiful and the unbeautiful in music, painting and architecture. It is

subject to the same advancing taste characterizing the evolution of a progressive people, and the standards of beauty which govern its colors and combinations are, as in the arts, founded on the majority opinion of those who know.[11]

Heckel believed that "those who know" were the paint manufacturers, the architects, and the painters. If those three groups could agree on colors, or combinations of colors, which would represent the "best taste," they would be able to convince the public of their validity and dictate trends in house painting.[12]

The committee planned to focus the campaign towards women:

In house painting it is women to whom we cater. She lives in the house twenty-four hours of the day. To her husband it is a place of lodging and recreation. Her taste, then, is normally dominant, not only regarding the form of the house, but as to its dress. If we can guide or educate the taste of the house-mistress in respect to the colors in which her dwelling is to be clad, we control the entire situation.[13]

Heckel argued that women followed fashion whether it was becoming to them or not. If the garment industry was able to find success in dictating color taste, then the paint industry should also be able to influence the housewife, as it was she who selected paint colors for her home.

Several months prior to meeting with this Michigan group of architects, the Bureau had begun promoting copper brown and copper verde in popular magazines. The advertisements appealed to the fashion sense of women. A full-page advertisement published in *Collier's* magazine on March 30, 1907, captioned, "Spring Styles in Paints," included a color rendering of an upscale home identified as the "1907 mode"[14] (fig. 79).

8. The exact composition for the paints was worked out in the laboratory of the paint manufacturing concern of Heath & Milligan. They were Copper Verde: C.P. chrome green, let down to a 25 percent commercially pure green, and matched to shade with C.P. chrome yellow and ivory black; Copper Brown: Prince's Double Label Mineral, B.F. Ochre and deep para red.

9. Heckel, *The Paint Industry,* pp. 410–11.

10. Bureau of Promotion and Development, Paint Manufacturers' Association of the United States: Preliminary Booklet—Addresses on Paint delivered before the Michigan Chapter, American Institute of Architects, 1907, p. 47.

11. Ibid., p. 48.

12. Ibid., p. 49.

13. Ibid., pp. 48–49.

14. In "Spring Styles in Paints," *Collier's,* Vol. 39 (March 30, 1907), p. 27.

Spring Styles in Paints

The 1907 Mode

We all follow the decrees of fashion—we may be slow, but we follow.

Savage fashions never change—the difference is civilization. The same instinct that has brought us telephones, trolley cars and electric lights, prompts us to change from time to time the cut and colors of our dress.

Woman, more sensitive and more exacting than man, obeys the impulse first and most frequently—and with good effect—for the American woman is the world's best dressed.

This year the American woman, if she be right up to date, will wear a *Copper Brown* frock.

This year the American woman's house, if she be equally exacting as to her house's dress, will also wear a coat of COPPER BROWN, with a beautiful harmonizing trim of COPPER VERDE.

When fully clad it will resemble the plate shown on this page.

These two colors have been prepared by paint manufacturers to meet the demand. For the first time in the history of paint making you can get the colors you want from any first class dealer, without the preliminary argument with the painter to convince him that you really know what you want. You don't have to show a piece of dress goods and learn that it cannot be matched—it has already been matched and awaits your convenience.

The two colors come *in sealed cans only* and cannot be successfully imitated by hand mixing. They are made not only for looks but for wear and in buying them you'll get your full money's worth in service as well as in beauty.

Have your own way this time, buy the paint and have the painter apply it properly.

A pamphlet full of useful paint information sent free to any property owner by the Paint Manufacturers' Association of the U. S., 634-636 The Bourse, Philadelphia, Pa.

27

79. *"Spring Styles in Paints," Collier's Vol. 39, March 30, 1907: 27. Courtesy of The Enoch Pratt Free Library, Baltimore, MD.*

The advertisement stated:

> Woman, more sensitive and more exacting than man, obeys the impulse first and most frequently—and with good effect—for the American woman is the world's best dressed. This year the American woman, if she be right up to date, will wear a Copper Brown frock. This year the American woman's house, if she be equally exacting as to her house's dress, will also wear a coat of COPPER BROWN, with a beautiful harmonizing trim of COPPER VERDE.

The ad was run solely by the Association, and no specific manufacturers or brand names were mentioned. Thus, the advertisement was intended to promote only the colors.

In May, the Bureau ran a two-page advertisement in the *Saturday Evening Post* under the caption "Good Paint Is Life Insurance for Buildings"[15] (fig. 80). Using similar propaganda, this advertisement noted that

> Fashion means civilization. Only civilized peoples have fashions in dress or in paints. For house painting this year, fashion . . . decrees COPPER BROWN and COPPER VERDE. . . . Look at the picture, shut your eyes and "try on" this dress for your own house . . .

These advertisements were clearly attempting to coerce the housewife to associate paint with fashion.

Members of the Bureau were enthusiastic about the success of their initial experiment. Heckel noted in a speech that close to 100,000 gallons of the two colors were sold during the first year.[16] With the assistance of a committee of master painters, the Association instituted a more formal campaign in 1908.[17] A booklet entitled *Fashions in House Painting* was published that same year. It contained drawings by architects of homes painted in seven harmonious combinations of hues

selected by the Bureau. All of the paints had appealing and picturesque names: Oak Leaf Brown, Couleur-au-lait, Moss Green, Ivy Green, Scotch Gray, Athole Green, Maple Leaf Red, Edelweiss White, Silver Gray, and Old English Brown, along with Copper Brown and Copper Verde.[18] A total of 100,000 copies of the booklet circulated. John Dewar, a master painter from Pittsburgh, helped develop the campaign and was so zealous about the ad that he paid the architect's fee for the renderings for the book with his own personal funds.[19] Advertisements were developed with the caption "A New Dress for Your House." The piece was illustrated with a well-dressed woman reading a copy of *Fashions in House Painting* and standing in front of a large suburban house (fig. 81). The text noted,

> A fashionable dress—fitted to its architectural form. It will cost you no more to paint it tastefully and appropriately than to take chances. A booklet on House Fashions, showing correct color combinations, suitable for all styles of architecture, selected by a committee of prominent painters, paint manufacturers, and architects [is available for free] . . .[20]

The message certainly inferred that the colors were selected by true authorities and that they represented the latest fashion.

In spite of the enthusiasm of the Bureau members, the experimental campaign was discontinued at the end of 1908. Heckel, in his history of the paint industry, offered two possible reasons for its failure: Either the industry was not sufficiently organized to carry the campaign to success or the campaign failed to establish a demand for the high-grade products that were promoted along with the fashionable colors.[21] It is apparent, however, that major shifts in promotional

15. In "Good Paint Is Life Insurance for Buildings," *Saturday Evening Post*, Vol. 179 (May 25, 1907), pp. 16–17.

16. Bureau of Promotion and Development, Addresses on Paint, p. 50.

17. Heckel, *The Paint Industry*, p. 411.

18. Ernest Trigg, "Fashions in House Painting," *American Paint and Oil Dealer*, Vol. 1 (November 1908), p. 14.

19. Heckel, *The Paint Industry*, p. 411.

20. In "A Fashionable Dress," *Saturday Evening Post*, Vol. 181 (September 12, 1908), p. 37.

21. Heckel, *The Paint Industry*, pp. 410–11.

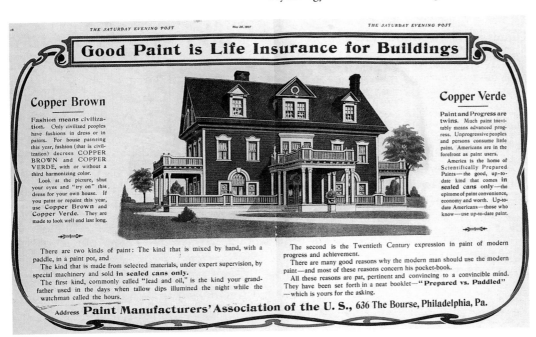

80. *"Good Paint Is Life Insurance for Buildings,"* Saturday Evening Post, *Vol. 179, May 25, 1907 pp. 16–17. Courtesy of the Library of Congress.*

strategies and programs by various manufacturing concerns after 1908 were directly influenced by the campaign. Firms parroted the original color recommendations and forecasted their own colors whether they were members of the trade association or not.[22] Manufacturers established decorating departments that offered free advice to the homeowner. Elaborate decorating books were published by many of the companies. For example, in the fall of 1908, the Mound City Paint and Color Company published *The House Beautified,* illustrated with color renderings. Also in 1908, the Sherwin-Williams Company established its decorative department and in 1910 issued its extensive book *Your Home and Its Decoration.* That same year an intricate book, *Correct Color Schemes,* was published by the National Lead Company.[23]

The years 1907 and 1908, therefore, represent a turning point for advertising and promotional strategies within the paint industry. As a result of the activities that began during this period, the coordinated efforts of the paint manufacturers brought them into the role of color tastemaker, replacing the individuals who had relayed their recommendations in an unsystematic and haphazard manner during the nineteenth century.

Members of the paint manufacturing industry continued to function as color tastemaker for American domestic architecture until the early 1920s. Then, firms from various branches of the paint industry began to purchase their color forecasts from the Color Association of the United States.[24] This group was incorporated in 1915 for the purpose of recommending colors to the manufacturers of ladies' garments. The early forecasts by the group were so successful, however, that manufacturers of numerous products not related to the garment industry also began to follow their recommendations. To this day, CAUS, along with a handful of other committees and individual forecasters, continues to lead American industry in its color selections.

---

22. "Spring Paint Styles," *The S.W.P.,* Vol. 4 (April 1907), p. 58. Published by the Sherwin-Williams Company, Cleveland; interview with Patricia Eldredge, Archivist, the Sherwin-Williams Company.

23. *House & Garden,* Vol. 14 (September 1908), p. 17; O.C. Harn, *Correct Color Schemes* (New York: National Lead Company, 1910); William Clendenin, *The House Beautified* (St. Louis: Mound City Paint and Color Co., 1908); *Your Home and Its Decoration* (Cleveland: The Sherwin-Williams Company Decorative Department, 1910).

24. Unpublished records (membership lists) of the Color Association of the United States. Located at the Hagley Museum and Library, Wilmington, Del., Manuscripts Division.

A NEW DRESS for YOUR HOUSE

A fashionable dress—fitted to its architectural form. It will cost you no more to paint it tastefully and appropriately than to take chances.

A booklet on House Fashions, showing correct color combinations, suitable for all styles of architecture, selected by a committee of prominent painters, paint manufacturers, and architects, FREE FOR THE ASKING.

The colors shown are supplied by all the leading manufacturers, and can be obtained through any painter or dealer.

THEY COME IN SEALED CANS ONLY.

The sealed can and the responsible maker's name are your guarantee of quality in paint.

Send for "The Fashion in House Painting" to
BUREAU OF PROMOTION AND DEVELOPMENT
THE PAINT MANUFACTURERS' ASSOCIATION OF THE U.S.
623-625 THE BOURSE   PHILADELPHIA, PA.

81. *"A Fashionable Dress," Saturday Evening Post, Vol. 181, September 12, 1908, p. 37. Courtesy of the Library of Congress.*

Part Three
Color Cycles in Industry

There appear to be different discernible color trends for different decades, as described from the 1960s to the present by Tom Porter in this book's introduction. During this century, noticeable shifts in color preference throughout many industries may occur at predictable times. From one product to the next, cycles of color change, and the repetition of color taste may vary considerably.

The fashion world changes its color taste approximately every two years, while interior design's period is considerably longer—seven to twelve years, due in part to its own considerations of economics and business. Color cycles are, however, particularly important to manufacturers of consumer products. As an example, the influences of color taste from the fashion industry to products are also closely observed to foresee particular relevance of shade modifications and best-selling colors.

In the automotive industry, color trends are followed very closely. Fluctuations in some car colors are well documented by sales drops, while other colors maintain relatively steady popularity. Many long-term studies conducted since World War II have provided manufacturers with evidence of the connection between popular clothing colors and product colors. This, in turn, has helped to provide manufacturers with the concept that colors proven popular in soft goods (fashion) are often also successful in hard goods.

Color Forecasting and Marketing for Home Furnishings

Sydney A. Sykes

82. *Printed duvet and pillowcase set with plain dye reversible quilt in Dorma's 1992 Home Furnishings Collection, with matching reversible pillowcases with studs as a new product development to give a totally reversible look. Photo courtesy of S. A. Sykes, Dorma, Coats Viyella Home Furnishings Ltd.*

This season's trendy colors, designs, shapes, and styling are more than a designer's whim; they reflect social change, global economics, technological advancements, and much more. When designers decide and discuss trends in home furnishings, or even cosmetics and clothes, they often sound more like economists.

Good designers are a reservoir for information, storing and reflecting the most important things they see and hear; they are thirsty for and receptive to ideas from films, art, books, TV, people, and technology. They must at first accept everything and then slowly reject, peeling back the irrelevant layers of unusable material, until they

83. *A beautiful hand-embroidered tape lace from China on Dorma's "Cotton-Rich" percale. Luxury and value give sophisticated elegance to the bedroom. Photo courtesy of S.A. Sykes, Dorma, Coats Viyella Home Furnishings Ltd.*

arrive at the focused essence of a new direction, style, color, or product. This provides a "focus," which may, in turn, become a trend.

Not all directions in style are risky or adventurous. To foster continued success in home furnishings in today's recessionary times, when customers require quick response, shorter product cycles, value-added merchandise, differential product and styling, the traditions of yesteryear and traditional old-fashioned values are a reassurance to most nostalgic customers. We regress to living according to our common heritage, and if we stick to this proven philosophy, the products surrounding us display an easy

84. *Deep, rich Hispanic derivative in Dorma's 1992 Bedwear "Portfolio" Collection, designed by S. A. Sykes. Photo courtesy of S. A. Sykes, Dorma, Coats Viyella Home Furnishings Ltd.*

acceptance, as little or nothing will offend the eye.

New market directions, therefore, will always comprise a good dose of romance, mixed with a cocktail of nostalgia, a high degree of crafts-manship and simple elegance, volumes of charm, a modicum of wit—mixed and blended with memories of a bygone age and the inheritance it embraces. Add to all these ingredients the talents of today's artists and designers, who, with flair and

creativity, fuse these energies with style and color to create new looks, new directions, and new trends.

It is not, however, the ivory-towered designer who succeeds as a loner these days, because manufacturers and retailers continue to work more closely together, as buyers and suppliers fuse to create a closer cooperation and understanding, not only at home but by international licensing that

85. *Fully coordinated bed linen range in Dorma's 1992 collection from the Silver Studio Archive, housed at the Middlesex Polytechnic in London. Photo courtesy of S. A. Sykes, Dorma, Coats Viyella Home Furnishings Ltd.*

gives a global portfolio to today's business environment. The "design here, build there" collaboration continues, as developmental costs are shared and the global map gets redrawn again. As trade barriers and commercial barriers are breached, and subtle changes in cultures and knowledge blur and refocus, the professional designer must rationalize these external influences and take account of numerous internal established considerations, in order to best change direction so as to gain maximum acceptance of new style or direction. Product costs, be it fiber or finished material printing techniques and sewing technology, are the practical parameters that may have to be questioned, if change is to come.

Color is still the primary purchasing consideration; a change in color is often the first obvious indicator of a new season's palette. Each year will have its essential throwaway colors, but a good design with a durable, timeless quality best reflects maturity in the marketplace. It can be summed up as "Fashion is fickle, but good classic design lasts forever."

However, the greater the risk the greater the rewards, and the skill is in finding a new direction and having the authority and confidence to break away from the constraints of conservative traditions, yet to retain quality and aesthetics previously taken as a given, and allow the creative framework to be flexible to promote change—"to stay ahead you have to look ahead."

New directions will only happen if a product is possible and probable, and there is a persuasion to do it. Also you need a creative team of people, with the correct priority to produce a profit. These are the six principles to change when managed effectively by individuals or design teams. However, if not available or not handled correctly, these can also be the catalysts for constraint.

Designers today should experiment and create "close encounters with tomorrow." By trying out innovations that may someday be part of our daily lives, they should continue to explore new directions and tap into ideas for fueling our futures. The source of inspiration comes from yesterday's daydreams, today's good ideas, or a futuristic figment of their imaginations—they must blend them into new and imaginative creations, whether in home furnishings, fashion, art, literature, science, film, or graphic design. The colorful world of creativity fires our most powerful asset, the human mind. The designer is a careful synthesis for imagination's application to improve the quality of our lives. And as we speed toward the twenty-first century and a new millennium, design and creativity are precious commodities. In today's resource-conscious society, may I humbly suggest we don't waste a drop of this elixir (Figs. 82–85).

Color Forecasting–Mystery or Science?
Kenneth X. Charbonneau

86. *Pink, Rose, Mauve: We see the "Greyness" being removed from Mauve. When cleaned up, it emerges as Pink, specifically Pink into Magenta. Mauve is diminished rapidly, but still appears on our board as it will remain a mass-market item for several more years. It may have to appear as a "transitional" bridge color in wallcoverings and fabrics, as was Beige ten years ago. Courtesy of Kenneth X. Charbonneau.*

The business of color forecasting has certainly been a subject of dispute for decades. Can there be such a thing? Are there people and organizations who could possibly determine what color preferences the consumer might have several years in advance? It is totally reasonable to question this. Let's take a look at some of the experience that I've have as a "color forecaster."

Even the most doubtful people must admit that they have witnessed cycles of color within their lifetime. The one that most of us recall, and unfortunately may still be witness to, was the "avocado syndrome." What an amazing phenomenon this was. Hardly any visual item in our lives escaped the "Big Three"—avocado green, harvest gold, and coppertone. The biggest influence was in the appliance field, where thousands of

these rather strangely colored objects were ground out by manufacturers. An avocado green haze crept into and onto everything. Because of its phenomenal success in large and small appliances, every other industry that designed and manufactured items to be in or near the kitchen and bath had to adjust and coordinate its color selection accordingly. Although kitchens and baths in these colors were the most memorable, not a room in the house were spared. Fabrics, carpets, rugs, resilient floors, paints, and laminates began reacting to the Greyed-Green influence. In addition, there were orange, gold, and, unfortunately, "Mediterranean" furniture.

The next memorable surge was the infamous "earth tones." The first of the dark, heavy browns had, as no great surprise, a green influence. The

87. *Blues: The "Greyed" Blues are diminishing and will be replaced by Blue-Violets: Periwinkles, Cobalts, Ultramarine—all cleaner, clearer with a Red undertone. The classic Navy and Indigo will remain in the palette as they always have. Courtesy of Kenneth X. Charbonneau.*

color brown made the biggest impact. We wore chocolate brown (i.e., the brown, double-knit suits with white stitching), we drove chocolate brown, our office was chocolate brown, as were our favorite restaurants, and our homes. The orange from the avocado period continued along with terra-cotta and other warm earth colors. To relieve some of the heaviness, we had the "naturals" in the form of Haitian cotton fabrics, Berber carpeting, straw, rattan, wicker, and other natural materials.

Texture became important, which was a logical thing to happen. As the earth tones were rather limited in their range of colors, it became necessary for designers to hype up texture to add interest to a space. In addition to the Berbers, we had all kinds of handwoven looks—tweeds,

nubbies, and other coarse textures. Who could ever forget shag carpeting? Stucco-texture walls became rampant, along with dark, heavy, rustic paneling and beams. Many of us are still trying to "undo" these color and design statements. Interior and exterior colors and textures became indistinguishable. In addition to stucco, other exterior materials were brought inside: brick, slate, Stone, rough-sawn paneling, even exterior shakes were commonly specified for residential and commercial/contract use. Spaces became dark and cave-like. How long could we live and work in these kinds of environments? Something had to happen.

What happened not only was needed but made sense. Those of us involved with color styling knew that there had to be a relief from the dark, light-absorbing earth tone palette. In approximately six

88. *Purple Violet: a perfect companion for the Blue-Violets, a major accent color. It has emerged because Grey is now the neutral of the decade. We also include on our board some Red-Violets into Magenta; this is a link to similar colors emerging on the Pink, Rose, Mauve board. Courtesy of Kenneth X. Charbonneau.*

to eight years, what we thought was warm and cozy, had become dingy and depressing. The browns and earth tones had not aged well. We had to offer the consumer an easy way to lighten up his or her environment. At the peak of earth tones, neutrals, and naturals, Benjamin Moore introduced a collection of colors called "Garden Pastels and Romantic Whites." Although some of our dealers were resistant to the possible need for this kind of color, it had to happen. Pastels were the most logical way to add new life. Peaches, pinks, pale blues, greens, ivories, creams looked fresh and new against the chocolate browns and earth tones. Things began to brighten up. . . .

The next wave of color to sweep across the United States and Canada was one whose impact none of us could have anticipated. In addition to

the lightening up with pastels, colors and textures began to soften and become more "traditional." One of the big influences was the Bicentennial. We began to realize that the United States offered culture and history, and this influenced the home furnishings and contract market. Rather than our looking to Europe or Asia, *they* were looking to *us* for design and color. (The High Point, N.C., furniture market and the NEOCON contract market in Chicago are now attended by people from all around the globe.) We looked back and examined design and color from our country's comparatively brief history.

Traditional color influences were historically inspired. Our "Historical Color Collection" was introduced in 1976 for the Bicentennial and has continued to grow in popularity. It is a selection of

89. *Reds: The Deep Wines, Claret Reds, Berry Shades are the traditional classics that still continue on our boards. What's New? The "Red-Reds" that are so bright and clear that they have a distinctive Orange cast. Courtesy of Kenneth X. Charbonneau.*

rather toned, muted, "greyed-off" colors. Their richness is in their subtlety. "Williamsburg" shades of blues, greens, roses, and ivories are complemented with reds and shades of putty and gold.

A major design trend that evolved from this influence was the enormously popular "Country Look." The need for nostalgia grew, along with a return to Grandma's kitchen, her values, and our roots. The kitchen became the design focus, growing larger and more open, often a "Great Room" rather than a "Family Room." There was a desire for one large active space in which families could interact. Cooking and baking became family activities. It was even acceptable for Dad to demonstrate his culinary skills. These new lifestyle directions dictated not only softer, prettier colors, but more practical fabrics, fibers, and, in our case, wall finishes.

Traditionally, flat wall paints had been the biggest sellers in our industry; now there was a need for high-gloss levels that offered better washability. The stucco walls were gone and replaced by the eggshell, pearl, and satin finish products that were specified.

The big color success was grey, the neutral of the decade. When, finally, grey replaced brown, the doors opened to all kinds of beautiful colors to return to the palette. The first and most important were rose and mauve. Who of us could have fully realized that these would not only be highly popular for home furnishings, but would be specified for every hotel, restaurant, office, and nursing home across the nation? Rose, and mauve grey with a "touch of teal" have established themselves in less than a six-year period. It's extraordinary that commercial contract spaces and

90. *Coral, Shrimp, Peach: Peach has been much too popular to disappear. We may be "Mauved out," but we are not "Peached out." Its cosmetic qualities assure us it will continue for years to come. It has sold well for all industries, and may be considered a neutral, and we have also put it on our neutral board. Coral is the important story; emerging from the Peaches, it has an Orange influence. A fabulous color to combine with the "new" Greens. Courtesy of Kenneth X. Charbonneau.*

residences went from heavy, dark, "masculine" earth tones to softer, pretty, rather "feminine" colors and textures in such a short period of time.

But alas, this toned-greyed palette cannot last forever either. What is our forecast for the future? Here are some things to ponder; some have already begun to happen; others are just beginning to emerge (figs. 86–99).

Utilizing Information from Color Forecasting Associations

I am a longtime member of Color Marketing Group, a past president, recipient of its Dimmick Award, and designated Lifetime Member. It is an organization of such importance that I would not think of missing a meeting. No industry or

individual today can afford to be an island. Communications of information on color and design trends are essential to us all. We may have some strong feelings regarding color directions, but it is always better to confirm them with color experts from allied industries. For someone like myself to sit in my office and "feel" yellow greens coming back, without confirming that this is indeed happening elsewhere, would be very foolish. Today, our color cards and merchandising must reflect what the architect, interior designer, or consumer is looking for. Most people would agree that it is far easier to decorate a space today than it was ten or twenty years ago. Coordinating colors from industry to industry makes it much easier for both the professional and the consumer.

I am equally involved and supportive of the Color Association of the United States. For a

91. *Terra Nova: This is certainly the most important board in terms of a significant shift and change in the palette. It is the return of earth-related color. (Please note we do not refer to them as Earth Tones) The bases of these beautiful warm colors are the classics: Terra Cotta, Brick Red, and Cinnabar Red from the Orient. Although we quickly grew tired of the deep Dark Browns, these three traditional earth-related colors remain as favorite and usable colors. They are more important today than when they appeared during the earth-tone period. Also important on this board is the first sign of the return of Golds, Orange-cast Indian spice, and curry colors. Courtesy of Kenneth X. Charbonneau.*

number of years, I've been on the Interiors Committee and part of the selection process. Our committee is headed by Jack Lenor Larsen and has such design luminaries as Mary McFadden and Jay Yang. The Interiors' forecast card is very focused and has proven remarkably accurate.

In addition to the Color Marketing Group and Color Association of the United States, I regularly visit design centers and special markets such as NEOCON. These visits are supplemented by reading consumer and trade publications. A color forecaster must learn the art of observation. To forecast color and design, one has to learn to look at everything and everyone. The influences that effect change come from every aspect of life, including politics, television, movies, books, and personalities. Some questions to ponder for the years ahead:

1. What effect will President Clinton have on the country?

2. Will the business picture improve?

3. What style will Hillary Clinton bring to the White House? How much influence will she have on decision making—and on the public? And then there is Chelsea. . . .

4. Will global thinking and influences shrink the palette or expand it?

5. How different or similar is the color and design market in America? In Europe? In Asia?

6. Will the blockbuster Matisse show have made an impact on color and design?

7. In only one more decade, the baby boomers

92. *New Neutrals: rich, saturated neutrals. The most popular is the sophisticated Taupe family. Following these would be creamy neutrals that have a warm, creamy undertone, both "classics." The newest neutrals? Peach and Rose! When colors such as these have sold so well and have been so well accepted, they evolve into becoming and being used as neutral backgrounds. Courtesy of Kenneth X. Charbonneau.*

will be the largest group of seniors we've ever had. How will this affect color selections?

These are only a few of the questions that we must consider in selecting and forecasting color for the products of the future. Like anything, there must be a need for color to change. Very often it is because we are just tired and bored with a trendy color or color combination. Avocado and harvest golds, along with shag carpeting, died because the professionals and the consumers grew to hate them; the same with browns and earth tones. How much longer can we go on "mauving" the country?

Color forecasting groups help to stimulate the discovering or rediscovering of new colors and combinations. Their purpose is not to force a new color upon the innocent consumers, but to show them how new colors can enrich their lives. The one important thing that all color forecasters must keep in mind is that the consumer has the final say in the matter. If he or she does not like it, they won't buy it! Generally, it is the professional interior designer or architect who will use new color and design first. These creative souls need to keep exploring, experimenting, and looking for new ways to make special spaces. It is these special spaces that consumers see and then consider for their own use. We all flock to showcase houses and buy endless interior design publications looking at the creative new ways that interior designers and architects have used color. If color forecasters can satisfy the needs of professionals, then they have achieved that first step that may lead into a new color cycle.

93. *Green-Cast Neutrals: Without doubt these are the most fashion-oriented selection of colors—the kind of sophisticated colors that Ralph Lauren and other designers have used in both fashion and home furnishings. Included are Khaki, Sage, Celadon, Grey-Greens, Olive, and Olive-Brown. All are strongly reminiscent of Victorian/Edwardian colors, the Arts and Crafts movement, William Morris prints and colorations. A word of caution: These colors need to be balanced out with accents of jewel-like colors: Turquoise, Coral, Red, Pink, any pretty color that will prevent these shades from becoming too dreary. Large mass areas of these colors can cause the opposite effect that cosmetic Peach has—they can make skin tones look dreadful. Courtesy of Kenneth X. Charbonneau.*

94. *Yellow, Gold, Curry: The Yellow family has never been a big seller, but if indeed the color palette is "cleaning up," there is room for yellow. They range from the palest Butter shade to the brightest school-bus Yellow. The general rule for using them is the larger the area, the paler the shade, with the bright Yellows being used for Accent use only. More Golds are shown on this board, Golden Brown Golds with clean, crisp, sunny Yellows—a return of joyful color. Courtesy of Kenneth X. Charbonneau.*

95. *Black, White, Gray: Black and Charcoal are the biggest message here. In our almost twenty years of doing color trend boards, we've never had a grey board that was so dark as this. We are currently obsessed with Black and near Black. Because of this, White-Whites become extremely important again. They were needed to balance out the darkness of the Greys and Blacks. At Benjamin Moore & Co., we even had to review our top selling Off-White collection and "clean up" this selection. Greys demand cleaner Whites as partners. The most important direction for Greys is to the "cool" side: Blue-Greys, Steel Greys, and Green-Greys, Blue-Violet Greys. Courtesy of Kenneth X. Charbonneau.*

96. *Turquoise/Jade: The ever popular Teal family has shifted as well. Taking out some of the "greyness," it emerges as Indian and Persian turquoise—rich, more jewel-toned. Its peaceful, serene qualities will be important to us as our lives become more harried and complex. By the way—what is the* only *new car color on the road? Courtesy of Kenneth X. Charbonneau.*

97. *Garden Greens: All the Greens of nature are finally here. The foundation of our Green selection are the classic Hunter/Forest Greens. They have always been part of any complete palette. Also shown are mid-tone "Chintz" Greens, the kind that are often used with the beautiful Pinks, Reds, Blues, Violets of traditional flower prints. The range is extensive from the palest to the deepest shade of Green. This has been long talked about, but to date has only been shown in very small doses. In an age when people realize that some colors are not complimentary to their skin tones, it is not likely we will see large doses of any Yellow-Greens. Courtesy of Kenneth X. Charbonneau.*

98. *Pales/Pastels: This board best represents how we in the paint industry interpret and utilize color trend information. The sales of Whites and Off-Whites represent in excess of 55 percent of our business; then we address color. Most trend or decorator shades are custom colors; we do not have to be concerned about inventories of large quantities of colors, as thousands of custom colors can be made from just a few bases and an extensive selection of colorants. The bulk of our business still remains in the light pale end of the spectrum. Shown here are a new offering of "Fresco Pales," colors that are paler than pastels but still have a suggestion or hint of color. For years the most popular Whites and Off-Whites had a creamy undertone that worked well with earth-tone shades. Today we require Off-Whites that compliment all of the previous color trends we talked about. Here are pale shades of Periwinkle, Violet, Pink, Peach, Green, Blue-Green; almost all of the families are represented in this "Fresco Pale" selection. They look best when foiled against a clean "White-White", which helps bring out the subtle color of each. Courtesy of Kenneth X. Charbonneau.*

99. *Texture/Faux/Fantasy: The samples on this board demonstrate a most interesting thing that has happened to color and color styling. It has become more complex. For years we were able to talk about color trends, textures, patterns, sheens, all as separate entities. It's almost impossible today to do this as all of these elements are being used together to create beautiful special effects in fabrics and fibers. There is now a "layering" of color on color, texture on color, color on texture, sheen on mat. One element upon another adds a wonderful sense of detail. Further enhancing this look is the use of "Tasteful Glitz"—beautiful metallics. Gold, Silver, Copper, Burnished Metals are woven into or printed onto surfaces, adding to the sense of opulence. Even in the paint industry, the Age of the Faux and Fantasy Finishes has returned. Walls, which for many years were mere backgrounds, have now evolved into focal points because they are beautifully painted. Often creative designers take the wall treatment beyond Faux, making a one-of-a-kind statement in paint. Courtesy of Kenneth X. Charbonneau.*

Automotive Design and Color Forecasting
Robert S. Daily

100. *Color presentation in Du Pont Color Studio. Courtesy of Robert S. Daily, Du Pont Automotive Finishes.*

The automotive industry, like it or not, has had an intense effect on all of our lives. The shapes and designs of those masses of sculpted metal and plastic are ever changing, from year to year, as are the colors that adorn them. Color has a profound influence on new shapes when used wisely to deliver a mood, a style, or a statement of personality.

The various new hues and shades that appear with every new model year do not just happen by accident. With lead times as long as three years, they are the result of careful thought and planning by designers and color stylists. The development of automotive colors, both interior and exterior, requires careful research of coming trends, combined with the stylists' feel for what is right and what will stimulate the buyer. On the realistic side, the new shades must also be technically achievable, as well as durable and long-lasting.

Just as the graphic designer begins with a pencil or a sculptor starts with a block of clay, the color stylist must begin with the basics. Today, many of the advanced color trends begin in the arenas of designer fashion, interior design, and graphic arts. Collectively, these provide a sound basis for the color stylist to put together his basic building blocks. Further inspiration comes from the basic shapes and end uses or market segment for which the product is intended. Combining these ideas with the latest available technology, colorists can begin to energize their own creativity, conceiving new palettes and color effects that will stimulate the potential customer into making a decision to purchase. The possibilities are limited only by one's imagination, but choosing the right colors for the right products can be difficult and challenging, especially in the world of cars and trucks (fig. 100).

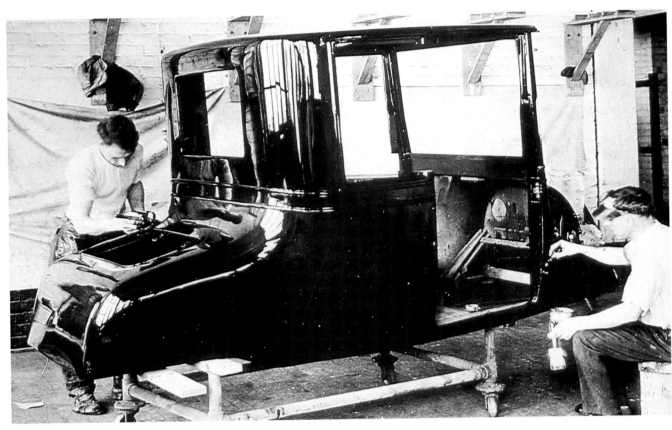

101. *Color being hand-painted onto auto body, early 1920s. Courtesy of Robert S. Daily, Du Pont Automotive Finishes.*

The history and development of automotive colors, and the trends that lead or follow, provide perspective on how automotive "topcoat" colors are developed and selected today. Color styling reflects broad consumer mood swings and the expression of those changes in automotive styling. Yet it is unlike other industries in that automotive color has been, and remains, dependent on technology.

In the early days, Henry Ford had his own idea about color for the Model T. "Any color you want, as long as it is black" is the generalization given to his offering. In fact, black was a wise choice in those early days of car building. Technology, or the lack thereof, played an important role. The only durable coating material for steel was varnish, which, out of necessity, was brushed on the body and frame surfaces. The entire finishing process took thirty days to complete. The masses wanted color, but it was mostly offered on the more expensive models (fig. 101).

That was true until the 1920s, when the Du Pont Company developed a product called

"Duco" lacquer for exterior automotive surfaces. It was durable, fast-drying nitrocellulose lacquer that reduced finishing time from thirty days to thirteen hours. That time was subsequently reduced to minutes, with the added dimension of drying ovens. Most important, it made color finishing on the mass assembly line possible, and the colors were richer and longer-lasting than anything else on the market.

Prior to "Duco," a production run of 1000 cars per day required twenty-one acres of covered space that held over 20,000 cars for an average of four weeks! The 1924 Oakland was the first production vehicle to use this new product, initially in "true blue" and later in virtually all colors.

The year 1927 marked the beginning of the modern auto as we know it today. Designers began to improve the appearance of their cars and their components, giving attention to overall eye appeal. Automobile styling would soon come into its own.

New ductile steels permitted graceful, sweeping "flying wing" fenders, adding to a longer, lower

102. *1938 Packard. Courtesy of Robert S. Daily.*

look. Metallic colors, those containing aluminum flake for sparkle, were available, although in a limited range. This gave stylists and designers a new dimension in automotive creativity.

By 1935, the automobile had an entirely different look. The trunk and gas tank were covered by the back of the car, and blended into the body. The radiator was hidden behind a uniquely designed grille, and roof lines took on smooth, rounded shapes.

Colors were mostly somber, dominated by dark, heavy-looking maroons, blues, browns, and greens. That is not surprising, given the status afforded to owners of upscale models. Sportier models, such as the very popular convertible, were available in livelier colors, including yellows, light greens and blues, tans or beiges, and, of course, reds (fig. 102). Color choice and its relation to lifestyle were being defined. With the dawn of the 1940s, a new sense of confidence pervaded the nation as it pulled itself out of the Great Depression.

Styling made a statement with torpedo-type body styles, bold grilles, and heavier bumpers along with the blending of headlights into the fenders. Promises of prosperity were abundant. However, all of that would have to wait, as the nation was plunged into war during the last days of 1941.

The postwar years brought about the peace and prosperity that had been long awaited by Americans. With them came a movement away from the cities to a place called the suburbs, and an unprecedented demand for cars. The age of the two-car family was born. The styling influences became even more modern, and color became a well-thought-out part of the design.

Color was used to lure customers into the showrooms. Bright shades were abundant, and multiple colors were the rage. The 1950s were the years of flamboyant two-tones, the debut of rear fins and high-compression V-8 engines (fig. 103). Even three-color paint schemes were offered, one of which was white, pink, and purple.

These colors matched other excesses in design

103. *Tailfins on a Cadillac. Courtesy of Robert S. Daily.*

such as spears, darts, and breast-shaped bumper extensions, along with double, triple, and quadruple lights mounted on increasingly outrageous "fins."

Paint and color technology showed modest progress during these years. However, your red dream car still had a tendency to turn pink in a couple of years due to degradation from sunlight. But improved acrylic resins appeared in 1956 and new colored pigments and pigment dispersion techniques allowed brighter, cleaner colors that were more durable than ever before. Superior aesthetics were made possible through a wide range of improved metallic effects, from fine and silky to coarse and sparkling. This era created the American love affair with the automobile, especially in California, where the car was a symbol of what you were, or of what you wanted to be.

By the mid-1960s, the youth market brought about by the baby boom was eager to explore new frontiers on wheels. Perceptive automobile visionaries brought us cars like the Pontiac GTO,

Firebird, Ford Mustang, Chevrolet Camero, and the Dodge Charger. The muscle-car era was born, transforming the basic mode of family transportation into a fire-breathing dragon of sorts.

Performance and image created a new set of criteria for the designers and colorists. Colors used on the everyday family sedan were too mundane for the muscle-car enthusiast. Distinctive color names such as Daytona yellow, lime rock green, hemi orange, and grabber blue were commonplace, and multicolored decals telegraphed even more of a personal statement.

The 1970s began on a theme of performance and ended on a note of fuel economy. It was full circle—back to function over form and style. Government legislation had its effect on colors as well, and designers found themselves without some of the working tools they had come to cherish. Automotive colors had to be formulated using high-solids resins; lead and chrome containing pigments were restricted in their use. The bright yellows and reds we were accustomed to were temporarily on their way out. But technology

104. *1970 Ford Torino. Courtesy of Robert S. Daily.*

answered the call again. New pigments were developed to fill the needs, and the resulting quinachridone classes gave us bright reds that were more durable than ever before (fig. 104). Color popularity in the mid-1970s showed that consumers were turning to the earthy, natural tones, with white the number-one choice for cars. But by 1985, white had moved down to third place in the popularity ranks, displaced by medium grey and dark red. Bright red became the most popular selection for sports and compact cars.

Current automotive design has evolved into a contemporary simplicity. The consumers' desire for elegance and sophistication is reflected in their choices. Yet, the countertrend is a renewed interest in individualism, despite the limitations of aerodynamic styling. Stylists are being challenged to create individual expressions of the aerodynamic form. Color will be a more important factor than ever before as a means to that end (fig. 105).

The advent of basecoat/clearcoat technology for automotive coatings has provided the stylists with a whole new set of working tools that enables the creation of colors, and color effects, that could not be offered in the past. The expanded use of mica pearl flakes has led to rich, exciting shades—even three- and four-layer pearlescent coatings that reflect multicolored hues (fig. 106). This, along with graphite and micronized titanium dioxide pigments, enables the color stylist to create unique new colors and color effects that had never before been possible (fig. 107). Traditional, more somber shades are being replaced with rich ruby-, sapphire-, and emerald-hued colors, due to today's ever-changing lifestyles and consumers' appreciation for the finer things in life.

These shades are a reflection of color trends first seen in designer fashion, upscale interior furnishings, and graphic design. From these areas, automotive color stylists sort out the first glimmer of emerging color directions. Along with analysis of current trends as well as those from the recent past, translations are then made into fresh color ideas for cars and trucks, and applied to the appropriate vehicles, all the while keeping in mind

105. *Pontiac Banshee, General Motors. Courtesy of Robert S. Daily.*

their intended use or market segment. Color trends in automotive design are evolutionary rather than revolutionary from year to year. By making wise choices, the stylists are able to enhance brand identity, while enticing the potential customer to purchase a product that is a reflection of his or her own personal style, or what he or she wants it to be.

Over the next decade, look for many new and exciting ideas to emerge from automotive design and color. Some of the possibilities are colors that change with heat or sunlight, as well as the use of holographic flakes that produce a multicolored sparkle.

There are hundreds of products that depend upon color as a driving force to stimulate possible new consumer interest. Predicting the correct hues and shades years in advance makes color forecasting a stimulating challenge.

106. *Buick Lucerne, General Motors. Courtesy of Robert S. Daily.*

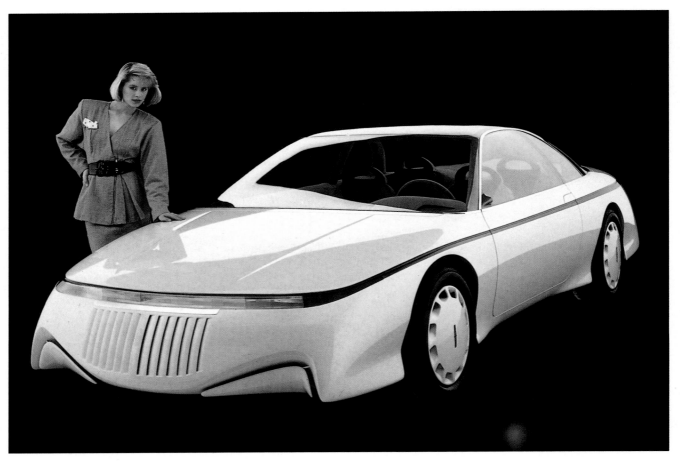

107. *Ford Machete, Ford Motors. Courtesy of Robert S. Daily.*

European Environment and Furnishings

Elke Arora

To speak in sweeping judgment of European design does not do justice to the actual given facts. There exists on the political and economical level a strong desire to standardize and create great conformity to design. However, there is an inherent contradiction involved, because Europeans increasingly define themselves, culturally and politically, in terms of the regions where they live. Also, designs from distant regions and countries outside of Europe intrigue consumers and are absorbed into the mainstream of design marketing.

Architecture

European architects have provided the design fields with a great deal of visual sensation and excitement in recent years. Partially because of a blend of Post-Modern and eclectic tastes, individual solutions to design problems have become prominent, varied, and have enlivened the European design world. Nevertheless, many public buildings still follow the mid-twentieth-century axiom of design: Form follows function. Administrative or public buildings have followed a pattern of intelligent design—wasting very little space, energy, and material. Residential design also appears to be efficient in concept, material, and space-planning for the working class. Many centers for public events have been designed in more elaborate terms of form, color, and materials, unlike their counterparts of the 1960s. Public housing and apartment complexes have been designed with a greater human experience in mind than ever before. Architects have become increasingly concerned with such issues as energy demands in the 1990s, focusing on solar energy, heat insulation with natural raw materials, energy-saving heating systems, and the reduction of water consumption.

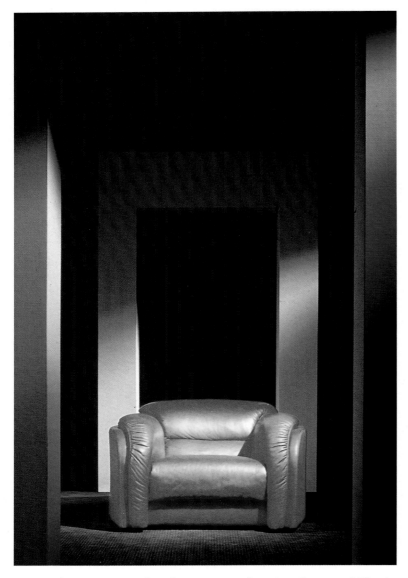

108. *Color accents in modern furniture manufacturing. Courtesy of Elke Arora.*

Interiors

In the realm of European interior design, people from all countries take special pride in owning, appreciating, and paying for fine furnishings. There are abundant variety and pluralism to most forms of design (fig. 108). Various styles compete side-by-side for public attention and interest (fig. 109). There is also strong interest in such traditional forms as Scandinavian, the "typical British," avant-garde Italian, "new Spanish," and the "known German" design (figs. 110–112). Each of these movements competes heavily in the marketplace for consumers interested in purchasing products with limited budgets, and each must accommodate all sectors of the buying public. Throughout all of these styles of design, there appears to be a movement toward greater domesticity, which is recently summarized in the term *cocooning*. From this vantage point there has also come a preference for muted interior colors versus the bright, "aggressive" colors of the previous ten to fifteen years (Fig. 113).

109. *Typical European color creation in a dining room. Courtesy of Elke Arora.*

A recent study, however informal, was conducted of architects' color preferences from 1960 to 1990 and included questions touching on spectrum colors, darkened colors, brown hues, pastels, the grey-white phase, and the new color chart. If one relates these color images to contemporary European architecture, one quickly discovers that pastels have been discontinued; the grey-white phase has increased and is dominant; violet (purple) is being applied in very individualistic forms of all types of design (fig. 114); and the new color chart (*Farbigeit*) is in the process of gaining acceptance with regional differences throughout Europe. Under closer scrutiny, certain buildings that were influenced by the Anglo-Saxon or Anglo-American culture show a strong trend toward the color combination turquoise-pink. The colors of European interior design come from all dimensions of the color wheel and, of course, are never intensive, but unobtrusive and elegant, reflecting the content of the new subtle color chart.

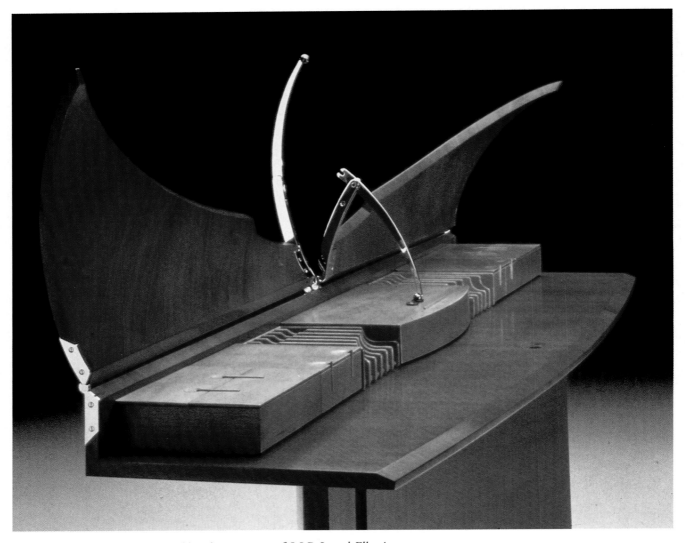

110. *Multi-functional writing table. Photo courtesy of S.I.D.I. and Elke Arora.*

Color and Product Sales

The shape, color, materials, and nature of construction in coordination with intelligent marketing strategy assist and determine the success of products in the European marketplace. Color and visual design have become increasingly important factors of successful product merchandising. With respect to function, the consumer appears to be fairly pleased. The success of products' visual characteristics, including colorations, seems more critical in terms of good judgment and, therefore, consumer acceptance and popularity. Color is the element that provokes a response of approval, rejection, or "Wow!" Color becomes, in a psychological sense, the language of the product, producing either successful cultural responses or creating barriers of language and culture to overcome. Color also affects products of export in a similar way. Successful colors in the European design market reflect a sensitivity in planning for the acceptance of regional and cultural diversity. Simply, successful products reflect the colors of the accepted region. Aspects of color psychology help to establish this regional image which stimulates the incentive of purchase.

111. *Classic chair of the "new Spanish design." Photo courtesy of S.I.D.I. and Elke Arora.*

112. *Classical exponent of the "new design." Photo courtesy of Elke Arora.*

Business Strategies

The key words for future business strategies in European design are *quality* and *service*. In the short term in consumption, goods of lower price range are marketable through sufficient quality. The higher-value market is meeting with increasing market consumer maturity, and in the long term, quality orientation is the best strategy. New products for existing markets have consumer preference ahead of new products for new markets.

Miniaturism, electronics industries, and products of human touch and sense have received great attention for further technical development. The intensity of research and development for existing products versus new product concepts seems to have the greater priority today. Areas in the marketplace for relatively high activity for new products include: video and audio systems, health care, sports, toys, vacation, entertainment, home

113. *The state of affairs: gaudy colorfulness. Photo courtesy of Elke Arora.*

furnishings, and do-it-yourself projects. In the product-development dimension, products that please older and younger people alike have attracted attention, with the trend of "Comfort does not depend on age" gaining wide acceptance. These include: large handles, push buttons, lever arms instead of revolving grips, automation at home, and gardening tools.

Consumers also want to be better informed on products. The effort toward consumer information is constantly raising the concern of the quality of life—not the quantity of life. The preoccupation with market product niches is a substantial dimension of present and future marketing strategies. The demand for services is growing. Many manufacturers try to coordinate the quality of their products with service. Companies are going to supply more intensive internal-service

114. *Excellent example of the use of violet. Photo courtesy of Elke Arora.*

Forecasting Beyond the Year 2000

offers and external-service offers, with the main thrust going toward value-added service and life service. A very significant dimension of future market planning is going to be a break with lifestyle-partition. The market will not be defined anymore by consumer groups but by products and their effective output for the potential buyer. In summary, the quality of products and service supply is the trend of future business strategies.

Europe is in upheaval. The European standard of value begins to rock. What was considered unthinkable four years ago is today everyday life. From these developments every country in Europe is affected. The British Royal House is exposed to public criticism—only a few years ago unimaginable. The evolution of Eastern Europe has also revolutionized our definitions of political and economic boundaries. Although old orders have fallen by the wayside, new economic and political orders have not yet replaced them. It is a time of transition and planning. Up to the year 2000, Europe is going to experience the birth of a new culture. This new culture will receive impetus from three dimensions: views of the private sector, views of social-ethnic relations, and views of spiritualism/religion. Rough edges of the outline of this culture are visible in glimpses today. Efficiency and progress are subordinate to the liberty and wisdom that signals an end to domination of experts and bureaucrats. An integral culture arises and a system of dualities is overcome. A public culture (pop, rock, folklore) gains a major innovative importance over the so-called high-carat culture (opera, theater). In fashion, these currents are already clear—the relevant impulses coming from the bottom and reaching the top in modified form and adapted. We do live in a phase of growing instability.

Many trends are coming into play. We experience the speeding up of communications/ information. Along with our burgeoning media explosion, the following tendencies appear likely for the year 2000 and beyond:

- Classical mass-economy does change an info-economy.

- New culture changes our consciousness and our visions for a future.

- Established counter-movements begin to alter/affect traditional values.

- Quality of products for segmented niche-markets, connected with service offers, are going to characterize the product areas.

- Reduction to the basic shapes and basic colors and connected planning toward "back-to-the-substantial" are going to accompany us on our way back-to-the-future!

Technology and Textile Design

Sue Ross

We are living in an era of incredible change. As the history books are busy documenting a new world map, new leadership emerges giving us increased awareness of lifestyle changes. Our concern for the environment and the economy, and our disenchantment with politics impose different priorities and positive action with an emphasis on education.

Cost, quality, and longevity become key issues in the marketing of new products. As better-educated consumers, we now demand more of manufacturers and their responsibility to both the economic and ecological issues of today's lifestyle. Although the cost of merchandise is expected to decrease, the cost of manufacturing will continue to rise. Manufacturers are faced with the awesome task of finding cleaner ways to create products that will live longer by nature of their durability, style, and color, while paying heed to the social responsibility of cleaner air and recyclable capabilities in the products that they offer. The cost of market research continues to escalate, as these manufacturers cannot afford to fail in a highly competitive product environment.

As an independent design consultant specializing in the development of pattern, texture, and color, researching niche markets becomes a never-ending quest for documented information of consumers' thoughts and market needs. Being right is the art of the service that I sell. Manufacturing clients, depending upon the product and its niche, expect at least a three- to five-year sales life as a return on the exorbitant investment they must make to develop, sample and market each new product line.

Keeping up with market trends and industry technology are equally essential tools to implementing new product design ideas. Analyzing the niche concept as it becomes a marketing reality clearly spells out the growing potpourri of style and design opportunities.

Managing the long wave of technology becomes an insatiable, ongoing educative process. From electronics to phototronics, micromechanics to phototechnics, we continue to develop faster looms and tighter weaves, equipment that creates more complex luxury items at affordable market pricing levels.

Computer compatibility is a must in all areas of design. Having started my own computer experience within the last nine years, I've grown from a basic word-processing system to a full-scale carpet and textile design program that requires a full room of dedicated space for its three monitors and three color printers—a system that allows for the visual prediction of color, pattern, and texture indentification that translates directly to the production tufter, weaver, or printer (figs. 115–116).

We know for sure that color is of equal importance to the design issue and to sales and marketing success. Learning how to interpret market movement is the trained skill. Keeping up with all current events, art exhibitions, theater, television, and travel are all a part of the daily researching process.

In the 1990s, we are surrounded by more color and design influences than ever before. Mixing cultures, periods, and moods has created an

115. *Solid Color Patterns: Mixing fiber types, machine technologies, and dye processing creates textural tone on tone prints via computer generated design. Photo courtesy of Masland Carpets, Mobile, Alabama.*

116. *Multi-Colored Dot: This cut and loop pin dot is created with mixed yarn types, color, and machine capabilities, resulting in a multi textural effect. Photo courtesy of Masland Carpets, Mobile, Alabama.*

extensive full spectrum of energized colors that encourage individuality and self-expression. Important to today's lifestyles is the need for more safety and security with increased interest in the quality of home life. Leisure and comfort have become a high focus of desire. More cottage industry with home work environments and the advent of home entertainment centers continues to grow, changing the way we think, work, and live.

All areas of industry are talking "eco," as the ecology issue blossoms full-scale, centering our attention and capitalizing on the naturals of life. Awareness of the sensitivity and effects of color and light stem from the research now being done specifically in the areas of the health care and senior markets. Understanding the healing effects of color and changing eye perception of the elderly have become an expected criteria to successful design solutions. We have evolved to an all-niche marketing concept as a reality of life. Viewing the needs of the different segments separately is now prevalent in all product areas. We look at the changing role of women, the youth market, the male marketing movement, and the greying baby boomers, all with a keen eye to directing design and marketing messages that will attract each area's specific interests. Selective, creative marketing now drives industry in search of consumer attention, ensuring new business opportunities for manufacturers, investors, and merchants. Integrity, productivity, quality, responsibility, and cost-consciousness are the new bible of design and marketing.

In such a fast-paced changing world of economic issues and trade agreements, the responsibility to research presents the need for new thoughts and techniques. Cross-referencing all products, including industrial, fashion, and furnishings, as well as within our own specific product environment, unveils the overlay effect that color and design have from industry to industry, product to product. Effects that help to ensure both immediate and future sales for the client depend upon the color stylist and forecaster's creative guidance. The reading, research, and networking never end. A full-time continuing commitment supports the forecaster's professional development and the ultimate success of design/ color concepts. For some, this theory is an overwhelming and tiresome process, but for me it is the welcome challenge of everyday life.

Designer of Distinction
Everett Brown

117. *Interior design reflective of an eclectic range of furnishings against a remarkably bright and deeply hued red background. Photo courtesy of Everett Brown.*

Everett Austin Brown is a fellow of the American Society of Interior Designers and has served the organization as chairman of the National Board and as member of the Board of Governers of both Northern California and New York chapters. In 1980, he was reappointed chairman of the Color Committee of the Color Association of the United States, a post he has held for a decade. As a nationally known interior design and color consultant, he was named "Designer of Distinction" by ASID at its National Conference Awards dinner in 1980.

His long career spans half a century of setting trends in his work with business and residential clients, creating original exhibits, model show-rooms, and national advertising promotions, creating public awareness of high standards in interior design. Born in Remington, Indiana, Brown started his career in Chicago in 1934 at Marshall Field & Company, moved his base of operations to Houston from 1937 to 1939, and later became nationally influential as color and design coordinator for the Grand Rapids Furniture

Makers Guild through 1950. As proprietor of Everett Brown Associates, Inc., offices were maintained in both New York and San Francisco until 1967, when his headquarters was moved to New York City.

Over four decades, many of us have felt his impact on American taste, whether or not we were aware of it. Throughout the United States, we have been in hotel lobbies, offices, and restaurants that Brown designed, seen department store windows and displays that he created, or bought for our homes his innovative floor and wall coverings, and his bed and bath designs. It is hard to define his precise style, but it is extremely American and eclectic, with emphasis on clear colors and comfortable furnishings (fig. 117). One of the many pies he keeps a finger in is the Color Association of the United States, where he has served as a past president and board member for many years. In an interview printed in the *Christian Science Monitor* in 1980, Mr. Brown commented on a question regarding his color precepts in interior design by stating,

Color, to me, is a vital ingredient of decorating. I use lots of it, but take care about how I distribute it in a room. I have always believed in the advantages of dark colors for walls—colors like bottle and olive greens, rich browns, teal and bright navy blues, and even black such as we now have in our New York living room. I once painted the walls of our California house all white, but we soon found them boring. I repainted the whole downstairs a fire cracker red, leaving white trim, and we liked that better. Darker colors are flattering to both people and things, but they can always be interspersed with lighter, brighter colors in other areas.

118. *Ameritone® Color Key Paint chart. Courtesy of Everett Brown and Ameritone.*

When working with residential and business clients alike, Brown discovers their specific preferences: modern or traditional furnishings, colors they like or hate—color is the omega of all atmosphere. As a former president of the Color Association of the United States and consultant to the Grow Group, Devoe & Reynolds on the Color Key Program (which makes it possible for the average person to enjoy professional skill when it comes to choosing the right paint colors for either home or office), Brown is well qualified to answer questions commonly asked of designers about how color affects people.

Q. *Why are some people happier and even look better when surrounded by certain colors?*

A. First of all, all colors can be divided into two groups or keys. All colors in Key 1 have blue or cool overtones. For example, a Key 1 red would be a rosy-pink red versus a Key 2 red which would have a yellow or warm overtone. A Key 2 red would be a peach tone versus the rosy red of Key 1. Think of rosy color versus peach color.

The coloration of individuals falls into one or the other of the two Keys, and it follows that their color preference will also fall into one or the other Keys. Therefore, people look and feel better when surrounded by colors from their Key.

Q. *How does one select those colors that are most compatible?*

A. By studying your own coloration (skin, hair, eye color) to decide which of the Keys you prefer. As you age and your hair and skin change color,

they change within the same Key in which you were born (fig. 118).

Q. *Can differences of a married couple in color preference affect their relationship?*

A. Ideally, a married couple are both of the same color preference, so they would surround themselves with colors of their natural and mutual preference.

Q. *How does the popularity of colors change as the mood of the country and lifestyles change?*

A. Fashion colors change with the seasons and with the years. For example, what is a fashionable color this year in all likelihood will become unfashionable as times roll on. Approximately every seven years the pendulum swings from emphasizing one color Key to being more heavily weighted in the other Key. For the past few years there have been more goods on the market in Color Key 1. Now more products are beginning to be manufactured in Key 2. These swings occur because leading designers sense a satiation with current choice and need to change. Hence, they go from one Key to the other, thus bringing about change.

Q. *What are some colors that were in style several years ago but nobody would be caught dead wearing now?*

A. First of all, manufacturers stop making clothes in colors that have ceased to sell. Some old popular color combinations, such as rust and olive green, plum and light blue, have long ago lost their appeal.

A Colorful Experience

Deborah Szwarcé

119. *Analogous harmony in a shop window on the King's Road, London. Courtesy of Deborah Szwarcé.*

Being a color analyst is challenging, stimulating, intriguing, serious, and fun, all at the same time! If you love to do research, to travel, take photographs, read, write, make files, consult with other people, and speak at seminars, then the rewards are many. Once I was asked after describing what I do, "You don't really call that work, do you?" My description probably sounded too enjoyable. I replied, "If you don't think that what I have just told you is real work, then let me tell you about the process of preparing a color palette for the interiors industry."

The key to success is to know your clients and to define their products, price range, and consumer. My company's clients include: manufacturers of every product seen in an interior—from wall coverings and furniture to decorative accessories, giftware, paper products

and appliances; retailers; fiber companies; the automotive and contract industries. It is vital to do your homework thoroughly.

And so the research process continues. When we start to develop a new color palette, we begin with a checklist of influences. The new colors will be introduced to clients in approximately ten months, and will be available to the public, or in products, about two years after that. We must track what the consumers are being exposed to and how they are reacting in order to make our projections. Our list may include: the social, political, and economic climate; environmental issues and organizations; museums; entertainment; regional and ethnic differences; types of restaurants and cuisine; local newspapers; fashion; what's selling at retail; global markets; trade fairs and periodicals; shelter magazines; architectural

120. *A rainbow of colors in Burano, Italy. Courtesy of Deborah Szwarcé.*

materials and style; or it may be just "something in the air."

During the year, trade fairs in every corner of the world introduce new designs for every category of interior product. In fact, we would be traveling constantly if we went to all the markets. My contributors, based around the world, and I cover the most important markets in the United States, Europe, and Mexico. There is always something to inspire us—it might be a new shape, textile, color combination, or a simple idea for a design concept. It is also a time to expand our vision and to exchange ideas and experiences with people from other countries.

One of the side benefits, while covering the trade fairs, is exploring the cities and surrounding areas. We try to allow extra time to shop the stores, take photographs, and observe the people

(fig. 119). Ideas come from everywhere. For instance, on one of my trips to Venice, a short boat ride took me to the island of Burano, known as "The island where the rainbow fell." And I saw why. Each building on the narrow canal streets was painted a different color. Bright, freshly painted facades contrasted with weathered hues— the soft, time-worn color of Italy. While photographing these buildings, I thought how adaptable these subtle chromas are to interiors, and they became the inspiration for one of our color stories (figs. 120–121).

Architecture is always a major source of inspiration, from the beautiful textures of ancient structures (fig. 122) to the instinctive application of color by unschooled people such as shepherds (fig. 123) and the vibrant color harmonies of contemporary architects. Mexican architect Luis

121. *The juxtaposition of time-worn chromas and textures in Burano, Italy. Courtesy of Deborah Szwarcé.*

Barragan has not only inspired me, but has also been an influence on other architects. His juxtaposition of vivid colors on the planes of his unadorned buildings captures the spirit of his country. When Barragan was asked why color was so dominant in his buildings, he answered, "For the sheer pleasure of using and enjoying it." (figs. 124–125).

The ever-changing colors of nature are another source of inspiration. I love the change of seasons, the way that sunlight and the atmosphere affect the landscape, creating subtle gradations of light and shade (fig. 126). Matisse often used windows as a design element to frame a landscape. It is an interesting exercise; look through a window or a door at the outdoors. Using it as a frame allows the eye to focus on the colors and textures within the line of vision and heightens the perception of color.

In the past, fashion colors were considered to have a direct influence on interiors, but the recent tendency in both industries is toward a lifestyle attitude. It is revealing to observe how people are dressed on the streets, or at a weekend activity, or when traveling. A relaxed, comfortable style is the norm, as it is in the home. Natural fibers, materials, and colors are desirable, resulting from an increasing awareness of ecology and the beauty of nature (fig. 127).

At the studio, after analyzing the enormous amount of information available to us, we start to develop the color palette by finding references for the colors that at the moment exist only in our minds. Through the years, we have collected bits

122. *The texture and natural colors of ancient stonework, the Colosseum, Rome. Courtesy of Deborah Szwarcé.*

and pieces from everywhere, of everything, which form our library. If we can't find a reference there, our search begins, or we paint it.

Because we deal with so many different products, we always think of color in terms of its end usage. It is almost like planning a wardrobe. Do we have the necessary basic colors—the background hues or neutrals for wall coverings and floors? Does the mid-tone range complement and work with the neutrals for textiles, bed, bath and table linens? Do we have the right values for accessories, or for accents? What is the overall direction? Is the emphasis on the mid-tones or neutrals? What is the theme, the identifying characteristic? Do the color names truly describe the chromas? These are just a few of the questions we must ask ourselves.

As a test, we then create color harmonies, thinking of various products and our themes, because we must substantiate our color story and provide our clients with visual references to design direction and product development. The themes may be based on a change in lifestyles, or they might involve a new direction in the use of materials. Whatever the influence, the views and needs of tomorrow's consumers are taken into consideration. There are no right or wrong colors; it's how colors harmonize with each other and how they relate to specific designs and materials that makes the difference. This exercise confirms the suitability of the palette.

To determine the future, we must take a look at the past. We analyze what colors have been successful for our clients, we study our notes from

123. *Instinctive color application for a shepherd's hut near Paesana, Italy. Courtesy of Deborah Szwarcé.*

the trade fairs and shopping at retail, and we review our color palettes from the past. These investigations are some of the ways to ascertain what color families are incoming or outgoing.

What does the future hold in store for color? As we approach the millennium, there will be an even greater interest in developing natural dyestuffs. In Como, Italy, Giuseppe Menta is well on the way to formulating ways to utilize natural resources. Organic colors will offer a new range of chromas. New technology, such as the further development of the CAD system, will change the way we perceive colors. Innovative ways to apply finishes and color, combined with the use of materials that are ecologically sound, will affect the design of furnishings. There is always something new to discover. But the bottom line is that individual preferences make the difference. Working with color is intriguing. Providing accurate information to clients is challenging, and every experience along the way is worthwhile.

124. *Pale color framing on a vibrant blue church in Mexico.*
Courtesy of Deborah Szwarcé.

125. *The use of two colors to accent simplistic architecture in Tlequepaque, Mexico. Courtesy of Deborah Szwarcé.*

126. *The bronze and amber hues of autumn inspire a warm color harmony. North Salem, New York. Courtesy of Deborah Szwarcé.*

127. *Natural colors and textures, accented with a bright hue, define the architecture of Val Varaita, Italy. Courtesy of Deborah Szwarcé.*

Bibb® Hospitality

Part Four
Color in Product and Graphic Design

The twentieth-century trend in product design has been to offer an explosion of color choices to the consumer in almost every product line. From paper clips to automobiles, five choices for product coloration at the beginning of this century have blossomed into fifteen or more available colors in a product line by the close of the century. Color has enabled many companies to develop products with strong images, instantly recognizable around the world. Consumers know the Coca-Cola Company logo by its color and dynamic ribbon form. Similarly, the Kodak logo, yellow tinged with orange and accompanied by black and red with other accents, has developed universal recognition. In product and graphic design, the challenge of creating a successful commercial color symbol involves the choice of the right hue for the right association and placed into an effective relationship with a product, service, or company.

The sensitivity of color selection to product visibility, appearance, and retention can be overstated and too strong, understated and ignored, or proven to successfully attach itself to the product—which, in time, makes the evolution of the color symbol more of an art than a science. From function to expression, the full . communicative potential of color in product and graphic design works on a variety of different levels, helping to create visibility, identification, association, and expression for all the products we color.

128. *Bibb Hospitality, Candlelight Tablelinen. Courtesy of Bibb Company and Leatrice Eiseman.*

Color Forecasting
Crystal Ball or Educated Choice?

Leatrice Eiseman

129. *Cosmetic color palette. Viviane Woodward Cosmetic Labs, Van Nuys, California. Courtesy of Leatrice Eiseman.*

For the last twenty-five years that I have been a color consultant/specialist, color forecasting has been an integral part of my work for a variety of industries, including table linens, vinyl flooring, color specification tools, office furnishings, food service, as well as the fashion, cosmetic, and interior design areas.

Whether I am called in to prepare color at the inception of a product design or to critique choices previously made, because lead time may take up to several years for many industries, it is vital to know future color directions so that a product or design will not look outdated too quickly. It is also important to know about the projected longevity in the marketplace and/or environment. Some

industries are more trend driven, while others must be able to sustain longer life in a product line or decor. This extends into other residual areas, such as product packaging, where the graphic design utilized must also reflect cutting-edge color appeal.

My work includes reviewing demographic background on typical and/or target consumers, knowledge about the company's image, sales figures, and popularity of current or previous colors, an overview of leading competitors' color choices, and consumer preferences, as well as the application and ramifications of color psychology. Color directions must be reviewed with all these and other considerations in mind; choosing colors based on forecasts alone is risky business.

COOL AQUATICS

130. *Cool Aquatics. Sample palette vinyl floor covering. Tarkett Inc., Parsippany, New Jersey. Courtesy of Leatrice Eiseman.*

I subscribe to several forecasting services, both European and domestic, as well as gather information from several professional organizations to which I belong. I serve on the board of the Color Marketing Group and this information is particularly useful and rewarding because of the Group's "democratic" approach to color forecasting.

Twice yearly, the CMG convenes at various venues across the United States and Canada. The membership is comprised mainly of the color decision makers in many industries. Our purpose is to hear knowledgeable speakers on issues impacting color, provide a forum for discussion on industry-specific colors for the future, thereby creating a meaningful forecast that adequately reflects the consensus.

Color forecasting involves an intrepid perusal of all the issues that influence color directions. The many areas to watch for signs of impending colors include:

1. Films and popular television shows, especially those in the production phase.

2. The world of music, specifically popular music, and the colors that the most visible or the rising stars are wearing.

3. Museum collections set for future openings.

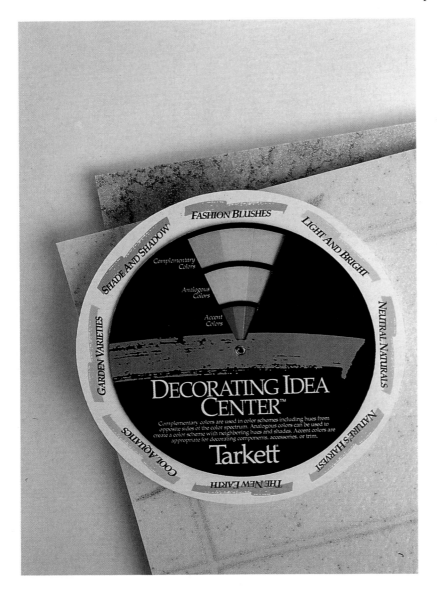

131. *Decorating Ideas Center retail display. Tarkett Inc., Parsippany, New Jersey. Courtesy of Leatrice Eiseman.*

4. Socioeconomic issues; for example, a weak economy may bring a more constrained use of color on "big-ticket" items.

5. Concern for the environment and a reduced usage of strong chemical dyes and pigments brings a renewed interest in specific colors, for example, the 1990s' earth tones.

6. Multicultural influences: Instant communication via satellite enables people the world over to view and use the colors of many ethnic groups.

7. Cyclical patterns: All trends travel in "waves," exhibiting a natural procession of high and low popularity.

8. Industry-specific trade shows, especially those of the acknowledged leaders in each field.

9. Political events—anticipated changes in governments, such as the dissolution of barriers between countries.

A strong trend often occurs when two or more of the above influences occur within the same time period. They may be anticipated or unforeseen. For example, in 1989, news of the upcoming film *Dick Tracy* and its innovative approach to vibrant color received a great deal of publicity. Of special attention was the hero's yellow raincoat, symbolically the modern-day version of a knight in shining armor.

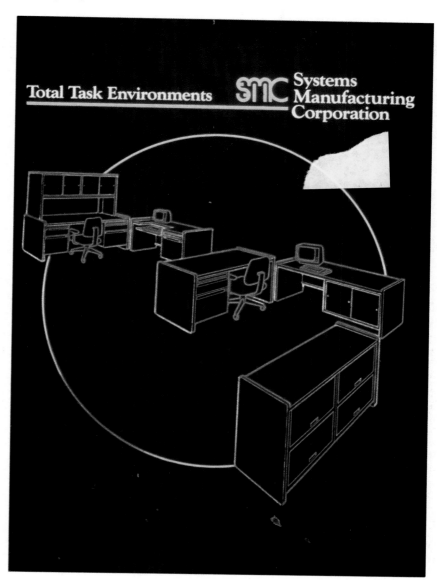

132. *Total Task Environment (Office Furnishings), Systems Manufacturing Corporation. Courtesy of Leatrice Eiseman.*

Several top designers embraced the color and included it in upcoming designs for 1990 and 1991. It was fresh, new, and timely. The life span of yellow was increased by what I refer to as an historical color accident. In 1991, the Persian Gulf war brought a flurry of yellow ribbons as a symbol of hope. This was an unforeseen phenomenon that could not have been predicted in 1989, yet it further implemented the use of yellow.

In conclusion, a crystal ball would certainly help, but because they are in short supply, a pragmatic, educated approach to color forecasting is not only advisable, but, in my view, absolutely necessary (figs. 128–132).

Color

Maruchi Santana

Amazing colors and color combinations fascinate me. In our agency in New York City, color plays a very important part in our marketing and design mix. Color is the emotional component of marketing; it's the thing that immediately, viscerally grabs the buyer and makes a connection.

Because of our location in Manhattan, many of our clients depend on us to serve as a "color antenna." They trust us to pick up the color trends even before they happen (because once they're

133. *Thematic Development/Product Design for the "Nefertiti" Clothing Collection, Swatch International. Courtesy of Parham Santana Inc.*

widely used, they're over) and capture these trends in our products and promotional designs.

How do we do it? First, we believe that color forecasting is not something that happens in some ivory-tower design world. Color forecasting happens every day, on the street, in the subway, in restaurants, in clubs, in school. You can see the future of color by walking down a Brooklyn street, going to a Queens high school, or riding the subway in Manhattan's East Village!

In other words, *people* do color forecasting; professionals merely notice it. You have to keep your eyes open. I am always amazed at how well put together kids are on the streets of New York. They're not rich and they usually can't afford high

fashion—but they don't need to, because they're creating it everyday! I make it a point to follow their trends very closely.

For example, well before earth tones hit the world of haute couture, they were on the street in beautiful living color. You'd see kids every day who were wearing an amazing palette of forest green, khaki, and tones of brown. They put it together from used clothing, army surplus, or Grandma's closet. Within a matter of months, these same colors were turning up in everything from pants to album covers.

The colors that kids spontaneously choose to wear today are the colors that forecasters will be recommending tomorrow. How do kids make their

134. *Product Design, Coca-Cola Watch Collection. The Coca-Cola Company. Courtesy of Parham Santana Inc.*

decisions? Music, the street, and the world and economic events, and growing awareness of the environment—the foremost concern of young people today. Young people wear the colors that make a statement about their hopes, their fears, and their dreams.

Right now, there's a growing feeling among some kids that the world is being united, and that all people can live together harmoniously. You see this hopefulness in the popularity of bright, African colors. I predict that this initial thrust will soon distill into a popular palette of orange, black, and green.

Color, then, is one way that people talk about what's on their minds. For a successful product or

merchandising campaign, it must talk to people in their language. When we design a product for the youth market, we not only observe them on the streets of New York; we also read their magazines, listen to their music, hang out at their clubs, and survey them. The same applies to any discrete market we're targeting: We "get inside their heads." For example, when designing for the boomer generation, we keep in mind that they're into nostalgia now. The pieces we design for them should have many retro-references and nostalgic colors.

People sometimes tell me that they can't have access to color trends, because they live in the hinterlands (which to many designers means any

135. *Package Design, Seasonal Packaging, Swatch Watch USA. Courtesy of Parham Santana Inc.*

place except New York). I say: Color is everywhere, and so is color inspiration. To be a great color forecaster, you have to think in terms of color. See color; make color a part of your everyday observations about the world. The color choices you make can have a great impact. The term *local color* has taken on a new meaning. The world is, indeed, being made smaller by global telecommunications. Local color can quickly become universal.

I think America is ready for a new color shake, a strong color infusion. Hopefully, our generation will bring a new vision. Here's to a colorful future (figs. 133–139)!

136. *Product Design, NASCAR Watch Line. National Association of Stock Car Racers. Courtesy of Parham Santana Inc.*

137. *Product Design, Textile Color System. Pantone Inc. Courtesy of Parham Santana Inc.*

138. *Brand and Product Development, Tennis Shoe Line. Japanese Shoe Corporation. Courtesy of Parham Santana Inc.*

139. *Copy and Design, VH-1 Media Capabilities/Sales Kit. MTV Networks. Courtesy of Parham Santana Inc.*

Beyond the Crystal Ball
Patricia Verlodt

Color forecasting is not an exact science, and like so many areas involving aesthetics, beauty, and design, color fits into an elusive category. There are no hard-and-fast rules that apply to how to color forecast, but there are certainly proven track records that show successful methods of the process.

Past Experience

Looking at a product's past history can add insight into how to forecast color for a future product line. For example, if a product line has shown that neutrals are the best sellers, tracking the depth of sales will provide information on which to base future decisions. Obviously you would follow a similar path as proven in the past with regard to other influences, such as the fact that warmer colors were purchased more often than cool and lighter neutrals did better than dark neutrals, etc. If a product cannot be manufactured in any hues other than neutrals, there is no need to expand your thinking. On the other hand, if new technology has allowed new colors, they should be explored. Some substrates require colors to follow a definite pattern, so that wood-like products would have wood-like colors and stone-like products need stone-like colors.

Gauging the time frame of a color movement in a given product area also determines color changes. Some products remain static for longer periods of time and others are subject to quick changes and shorter turnaround times. More often than not, slow-moving colors in product lines, such as exterior products and utility items, fall into a neutral color category of colors that are less colorful, low chroma, less trendy, whereas quicker-moving items are more subject to the latest trend colors.

Research

Every product is subject to its own rules and criteria for approaching research. The more information gathered on a specific product, the easier it is to select future colors. The first area to be determined is in the area of influence. Which product or outside influence most affects that product? This varies greatly from product to product and may include such factors as demographics, geography, who is buying the product, price point, raw materials, and dozens of other elements. Sometimes in the process of listing influences it becomes clear that color options are narrowed as well.

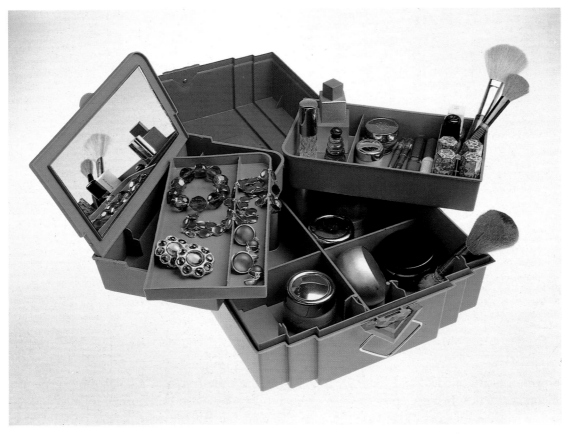

140. *Cosmetic Organizer. Sassaby Products, Photo courtesy of Sassaby and Patricia Verlodt.*

Experience and Intuition

It seems that experience and intuition are not at all related, but that intuition actually comes from experience. A "sixth sense" becomes part of a color forecaster's criteria for selecting colors. Proven methods can be reused and refined and become a valuable part of the color selection process. In fact, one of the most difficult problems a colorist faces is in predicting colors that a client "cannot see." These colors have no proven track record and do not appear yet in a given category, so the client has a hard time being convinced it is the way to go. This is where experience becomes a major factor in convincing a client that you know what you are doing, but most of all, once that confidence is proven, it makes it much easier to initiate the forecasting process the next time around.

Design-Driven Color

More often than not, color is design-driven, meaning it draws its influence from the shape, pattern, size, or texture of a product. Some colors translate well in appearance from one medium to another, such as from paper to plastic, while others lose their appeal in the process. A color that looks lovely in wool might look far less appealing in plastic or metal. Texture, depth, and geometry will often determine a specific color's usefulness. At some point the sheen or gloss may need to be adjusted, or pearl or metallic effects may help with the interpretation of a specific color. Just because a color is trendy does not mean that it will work in all products; but translations into variations of that color may make it work in other areas (figs. 140–141).

141. *Cosmetic Organizer. Sassaby Products, Photo courtesy of Sassaby and Patricia Verlodt.*

Color Trends

Besides relying on intuition, experience, knowledge, and other factors, there are color services that publish forecasts for specific markets. Taking these forecasts literally can be dangerous for many of the reasons that have already been stated. The application of trendy forecast colors is totally reliant on the product's use and usability. Color Marketing Group, a nonprofit organization of color professionals based in Arlington, Virginia, uses it's 1200-member base to determine color forecasts for the consumer and contract market. Unlike any other forecast service, it publishes *Color Directions,* which indicates in which direction color is moving, rather than specific colors. CMG members work on these palettes in workshop surroundings at semiannual conferences, but most members will tell you that the palette is not the biggest help in doing their own forecasts; rather it is the interaction of the members with each other that enables many to determine future influences that will affect their own product (fig. 142).

Specific Influences

There is a widely held opinion that the fashion industry is a major influence on forecasting for products and other industries of design. In my opinion, if color makes it through two or three fashion seasons and remains a top seller, it is destined to move into other areas of color, such as accessories, home furnishings, and related products. The sportswear industry highly influences sporting equipment, children's products, and youth-oriented products. Home furnishings colors can, in turn,

142. *CMG Workshop. Courtesy of The Color Marketing Group®.*

influence exterior products, paint products, and utility items. Peripheral product lines often influence each other. For example, ceramic tile, resilient flooring, and countertop products can be influenced by appliance manufacturers, and vice versa. Carpet and textiles may influence pre-finished wallboards. Products are linked together by a chain of color influences, coupled with each product's needs, and market specifics.

Long Versus Short Color Lines

Paint systems usually contain more than 1000 colors, which in some ways makes it easier to forecast. The difficulty is that these systems are in place for five years or more and, therefore, color forecasting the correct color families and the number of a color is tricky. A good solid foundation of core colors is necessary, with an emphasis on shifts in color preference being made with each update (figs. 143–144). To the uneducated, paint color shifts are very subtle and may include the insertion of more warm neutrals versus cool neutrals, more dusty shades or more clean shades depending on the color climate, while still including a little of everything for safety's sake. Short-term color lines are much more difficult and highly reliant on current color trends, and usually contain fewer colors as well. The effort to determine the correct "few" colors for short-

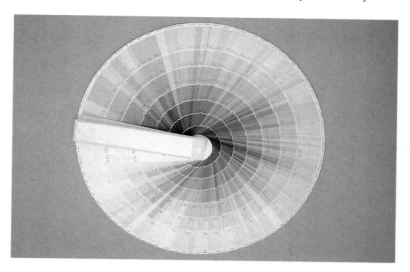

143. *Fan Deck. Courtesy of Patricia Verlodt.*

144. *"Color Symphony" Paint Card Display. Courtesy of M.A.B. Paints & Coatings (M. A. Bruder & Sons, Inc.) and Patricia Verlodt.*

term marketability relies very heavily on other factors already mentioned, such as past experience, research, and other product influences. One of my clients is Sassaby, a manufacturer of cosmetic organizers (figs. 145–146). This product is highly dependent on current and future color trends, as well as the design-driven shape. Since plastic is the material used, it is also dependent on selecting the correct interpretation of color trends to fit the product as well as the buying audience. Both the paint market and the fashion market have individual needs and markets; therefore, they have individual influences. All this illustrates the fact that there is not a given set of rules for color forecasting. Knowing your product, mixed with

experience, intuition, past history, design appropriateness, and help from those who may influence your product can make for a successful venture into the world of color marketing.

145. *Organizer by Sassaby Products. Photo courtesy of Sassaby and Patricia Verlodt.*

146. *Organizer by Sassaby Products. Photo courtesy of Sassaby and Patricia Verlodt.*

Posters

Michael Manwaring

147. Adopt-A-Book *poster. Photo courtesy of Michael Manwaring.*

Michael Manwaring established The Office of Michael Manwaring, a graphic design practice, in 1976, which has since developed into a multi-disciplinary design firm involved in print graphics, architectural signage, environmental graphics, furniture design, and architectural consultation.

With a clientele that includes both private corporations and public agencies, recently completed projects include environmental graphics programs for Rincon Center, a major mixed-use development in downtown San Francisco, and for Disney Casting Center, Florida. Current projects include Downtown Plaza, a six-block retail development in downtown Sacramento, California, and the San Jose Sports Arena.

In 1991, The Office of Michael Manwaring was awarded an art commission from the City of San Francisco for an interpretive project combining poetry and cultural and natural history, for The Embarcadero, a two-and-one-half-mile section of the city's waterfront.

In 1987, Michael Manwaring and architect David Meckel founded Environmental Image, a parallel practice specializing in large-scale environmental design projects.

Manwaring has taught at the University of California at Berkeley and Kent State University. He is currently an adjunct professor of graphic design at the California College of Arts and Crafts in San Francisco, where, in 1988, he received the Distinguished Faculty Award (figs. 147–149).

148. Under 30 *poster. Photo courtesy of Michael Manwaring.*

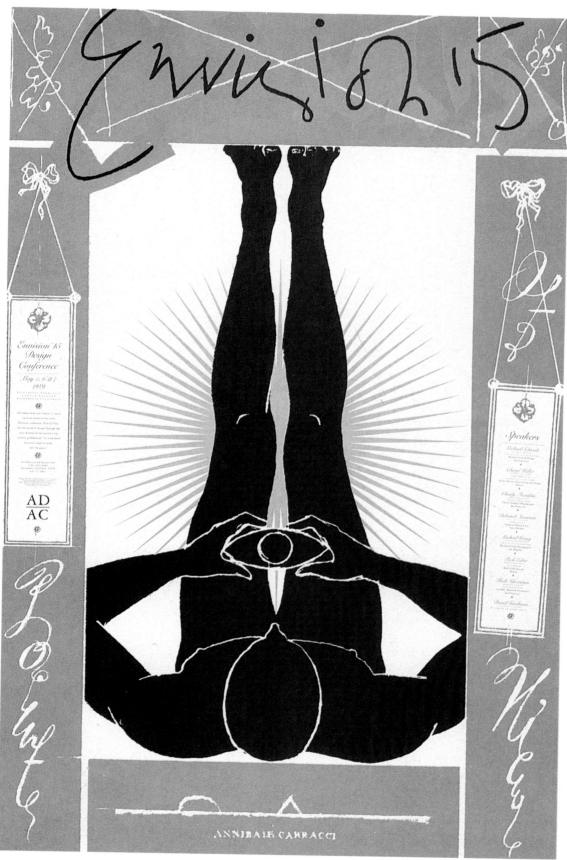

149. Envision 15 *poster. Photo courtesy of Michael Manwaring.*

NATIVE AMERICAN COLOR

Part Five
Techniques of Color Prediction

Can people and organizations determine what color preferences the consumer might have several years in advance? Although the business of color forecasting is layered with many different types of practitioners, services, and organizations, the most successful share several attributes. No matter how beliefs, methods, and techniques vary from one industry to another, they have developed a remarkable ability to simultaneously track multiple influences of industry, culture, economics, politics, and geographic events; maintain considerable libraries of reference materials, color catalogs, and samples; but most of all they have an unusual streetwise intelligence for finding evidence of coming influences and knowing how they will be assimilated into the various design industries they represent.

Confessions of a Color Tracker

Merle Lindby-Young

Color forecasting can be called the art of visualizing the invisible, and like the Native American art of tracking it brings intuition into play and all of the senses. The process is neither a mystical nor a market-driven conspiracy. In *The Tracker,* Tom Brown's account of learning tracking skills from an old Indian, the tracker's awareness is keen as he moves through the woods. He doesn't miss a movement, a sound, or a scent, though very little appears to be happening. These cues help him make conclusions about his safety, his hunting prospects, and his relationship to the earth.

The sights and sounds of change are less subtle in mainstream society today. Dramatic changes in our world filter down through political and economic structures, the arts, and the world's markets to the consumers, shaping their moods and choices. The color forecaster senses the nuances of change in lifestyles, environments, design and materials, and responds with changes in color. In my color forecasting process, tracking is the appropriate technique to evaluate societal and industrial shifts when nothing seems to be moving (fig. 150).

Growing up in the rolling hills of Hunterdon County, New Jersey, and influenced by my Cherokee heritage, I opened my eyes and my pores to the ever-changing environment. I was aware of the seasonal shifts in shape and color in the fields, woods, streams, earth, and sky. Nature's palette became my inspiration for color, color combinations, contrast, texture, and design. I learned to appreciate both the natural order and seemingly random patterns inherent in the outdoors. And I discovered that most successful color relationships had first been successful in nature.

Harmonizing work with life, I track as I move about in the international design world, on city streets, in regional shopping centers, and in the fields and farmlands of rural Texas where I ride my Arabian mare. I listen; I read; I watch the leading indicators and identify market directions. I put all of this information in my "color pot," along with the consensus forecasts of The Color Marketing Group, and cook it down to a personal color point of view.

Surface is a critical component in this mix; as a color and materials specialist, I cannot separate them. Color and finish together render a material appropriate for a given time. The right color for a product is directly related to the essence of the material from which it is made. For example, the only color that makes sense for wrought iron is black. Wood, however, can be any color or finish—natural, dyed, pickled, stained, painted, glossy, satin, or matte. Part of this is tradition, part is my own feeling about it. My view changes, as do the materials and processes we use to color them (fig. 151).

While traditional color forecasters, like futurists, predict what will happen based on facts and trends, I enjoy balancing hard information with intuition. This multidimensional holistic approach leaves no gaps in physical or sensory input. When connections are finally made between seemingly unrelated bits of information, the result can be a quiet evolution of the palette for a given period or a revolution of color and materials.

A brief look at the last thirty years of color bears this out. Peter Max colors flourished in the 1960s, exposing the ravages of psychedelia. International style was "in" and chrome was the

151. *Materials, Faux and Real. Courtesy of Merle Lindby-Young.*

noteworthy material. The "Age of Beige" followed through to the Bicentennial Year, when neutrals were replaced by the traditional colors—navy, hunter green, and burgundy. "High Tech" was the identification for the Industrial Expressionist aesthetic and a new appreciation for materials. In the early 1980s, we turned to a Post-Modern palette of greyed pastels and colored neutrals. More and more color options exploded into excessive color lines later in the 1980s until the industry cried out, "Enough!" Recycling color became more desirable than continuing the madness.

Looking back like this gives me a realistic perspective as I begin to forecast color directions three or four years out. Although some colors travel in cycles, the new interpretations are never the same as their predecessors. Even when similar, they are fresh and exciting in a new context. It is not merely my instinct that reinterprets nature in the colors of the 1990s. Supporting the need for bringing the outdoors into the interior landscape are such environmental issues as pollution and the endangered ecological balance. Natural designs and colors are synonymous with our needs and compatible with our ecological sensitivity. Using the colors of the earth makes an eloquent statement about this movement in time.

Color palettes for the 1990s will be more minimal as a direct reaction to the excessive choices of the previous decade, supplemented by custom color programs (fig. 152). If a designer wants a signature red, for example, it can be specified as a custom color. The entire gamut of greens dominate the forecast, responding to the "green" awareness that stems from environmental issues. Yellowing of the palette is influenced by New Age awareness and its relationship to Eastern thought—the inner power of the individual, connection to the universe, and inner glow.

Working across market segments gives me an opportunity to do high-end colors (avant-garde, daring, leading-edge, fashionable) for upscale furniture and fabric and to complement these with more basic palettes for building products, a market where product life spans are longer and color serves as a background. In a variety of applications, my unique color view appears as a unifying single thread. A color that may be ideal as a solid accent color for general office seating, for example, may be just one component in a space-dyed yarn for carpet or patterned upholstery. This is where instinct comes to the fore. Although separate design projects may have been independently influenced, they will be compatible when specified and viewed together in contract interiors. This may not have been the goal. It is always, to my continual amazement, a natural consequence of the process. No mystery. No conspiracy.

152. *Color Forecast for the 90s. Courtesy of Merle Lindby-Young.*

Colourcast Services

*Darlene Kinning**

Predicting and forecasting color trends does not require a crystal ball. It requires a dedication to a continual and ongoing observation of design and color directions throughout the world. It means that one is always cognizant of appealing new and recycled color combinations, noticing how they relate to the new or recycled designs. Pay particular attention to trends that enhance existing popular products' colors. Explore historical tendencies and note their repetitious rhythms.

Dramatic shifts in color directions from one predominant set of colors, such as blue and mauve, to another with an entirely different feeling, such as yellow, yellowed reds, and green, are always introduced by high-profile industries, given a theme, and promoted with much fanfare. These are the forecast colors. There will now be a quiet time while other industries—larger manufacturers dependent upon mass appeal—access the changes, create other themes to fit their customers, and reintroduce the same set of color directions. These are emerging colors. Allow a few more years of popularity for the colors to become established, and the cycle begins again. Sometimes a color trend remains in place while the period trend moves on. Southwest colors became Spanish Mediterranean, 1960s revival, and Lodge, while the colors—all influenced by yellow—are the same.

All of these factors are taken into account while gathering and writing Colwell Industries' annual forecast of color, *Colorcast*™ (fig. 153). Swatches of forecast colors from all industries, including home furnishings, fashion apparel, and automotive, are perused before narrowing the colors that will

*Colourcast Services' Darlene Kinning is the owner and a consultant and color stylist for Colwell Industry companies.

153. *Colorcast™ '94. Courtesy of Colourcast Services/Colwell Industries.*

project the color and design trend story. Affiliation with The Color Marketing Group and the London-based International Colour Authority directly affect the final choices.

Colorcast, published for Colwell Industries clientele only, enables our manufacturing customers to select, test for compatibility, and produce potential trend colors in concert with other related industries. The consumers then are able to create coordinating-color schemes throughout, inside, and outside the house.

Paint Color Systems

Not so long ago, colors for paint were limited and offered on a single card located at the paint store counter. You chose a color, the paint was mixed on the spot. Today's consumer has thousands of color choices, swatched on take-home cards to assist in the matching with, or creation of, new color schemes. These collections of color are offered by paint manufacturers to stimulate interest in buying

their paint. Colors, multiple-striped or single chips, are attractively arranged in well-lit displays and positioned as the focal point of interest in the paint departments.

Specialists at Colwell General Inc., in the production of paint color systems, make the color selection card and chip. Each formulated color is computer matched, coated, identification printed, packaged, and shipped per the manufacturers' specifications. Colwell Industries offers full design services that include consultants for color selection, arrangement, and name identification.

Before conceptual design and color selection can begin on a full paint color system, a meeting with the paint manufacturer is held to establish guidelines. The following details will be discussed:

1. Present system's evaluation and comparison with universal color notation systems, as well as with the paint manufacturer's competitors. Strengths and weaknesses are noted.

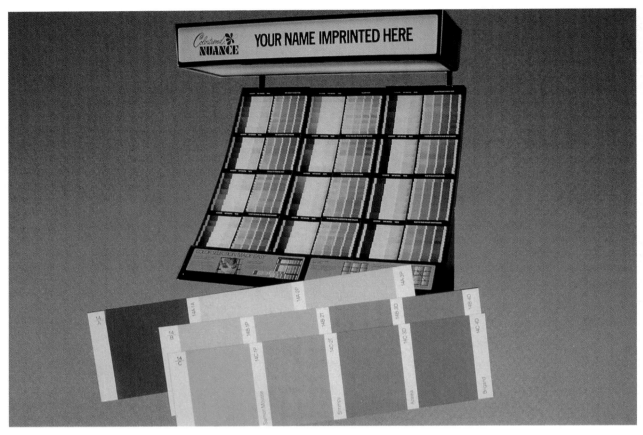

154. *Colortrend Nuance, paint color system. Courtesy of Colourcast Services/Colwell Industries.*

2. Establish the total number of colors for new system, plus

3. How many existing colors will carry over to the new system.

4. Will base and colorant modifications dictate a total makeover?

5. Size requirements for the display. This affects the card's size and number of colors per card.

The two paint color systems illustrated differ conceptually, while both maintain a balanced chromatic palette. The title refers to the color collection, and because they are syndicated color systems, they will be customized with a paint manufacturer's name.

Colortrend NUANCE has 858 colors, grouped into 78 concise families of 11 monochromatic shades, displayed on 7″ by 2″ cards (fig. 154). A key accent color boldly defines each family and is the lead into the remaining 10 hues that are subtle variations on the accent. The 78 families are grouped into six hue sections of red, orange, yellow, green, blue green, and blue purple. Within each section one can find seven sets of clear-to-muted hues, plus six sets of related near-neutral shades, offering accurate familial selections. Appropriately, the name NUANCE means "a shade of difference."

With Colortrend AMBIANCE, we were seeking a very ambient flow of color where every chip connects to its neighbor (fig. 155). It has its beginnings in our trademarked notation system, Colorcurve.® This computer analysis system allowed for evenly spaced and notated colors so that we were able to eliminate gaps in the palette. AMBIANCE epitomizes the color wheel in space. While yellow tops and blue ends each column, the steps in between are precisely split warm and cool.

155. *Colortrend Ambiance, paint color system. Courtesy of Colourcast Services/Colwell Industries.*

On the right are colors warmed by red and to the left are colors cooled by green. Earthy shades form a neutral zone down the center. The sophistication of this system lies in the interrelation of hue families and in its perfect chromatic sequence. Set into a convex display with clear viewing BIAX lighting, this system's rainbow AMBIENCE glows.

Research indicated a desire for large swatches of color, especially for light whites and tints. Both systems reflect this differently. AMBIANCE is totally committed to a lightened, soft palette with very large swatches of off whites and tints. Nuance bright accents become call outs to draw attention to the color's family and corresponding large swatches of off whites and tints.

Color Names

Giving names to colors takes imagination and stacks of reference books. I have been chagrined to

select the perfect color, only to have it rejected because the name is wrong. Laguna Beach is not right on a color card featuring Eastern historical colors, just as the name avocado has been "death" for products in the United States since the 1980s and 1990s. I really do try to choose usable and fitting names that can appeal to the buyer's image of the finished space receiving the paint or product. Take an ordinary grey, for example, and name it Garden Path, or Braintree Road, for thoughts of days gone by. Or pick from yellows named Spinning Silk or Softly Lit for a romantic touch. Understanding the demographics of one's customer, the application of the product, and the end user is essential.

Color Cards

Color cards are to showcase a manufacturer's product. They can also be used to assist the

156. *An exterior color combination color card. Courtesy of Colourcast Services/Colwell Industries.*

consumer in color scheming, for interior or exterior application (fig. 156). This card's chips are proportionally displayed to suggest a main siding color, a trim, and an accent color. The colors on the card are usually a collaboration between a manufacturer's data of current sales and a stylist/consultant's knowledge of future trends. Color cards are great vehicles for introducing new color and design trends. They can be quickly published and updated with fresh choices reflecting current colors.

Color selection and coordination require the hand of a color stylist/consultant who is not only aware of but familiar with consumer expectations. It is a full-time occupation that I love.

Pat Tunsky, Inc.

Patricia A. Tunsky

After twenty-three years of forecasting for the textile and apparel industry, twenty years of which have been spent in my own business, I am more convinced than ever that people cannot live in a world without color. A beige world or a black-and-white world would be nonstimulating, producing human stereotypes.

Color is a form of self-expression. In the form of apparel, it represents the way you feel about yourself that day. If you are in a positive mood, you will wear such bright colors as reds, oranges, yellows, magentas, jades, chartreuses. If you are feeling more introverted, you will most likely put on black, charcoal, navy. Psychologically, you will feel as though you are safer, more protected in darker, subdued color. Over the years, the successful professional has always worn the traditional dark "Brooks Brothers" suit.

The 1960s and 1970s brought about a new freedom in the way we dress and the colors we wear. In the 1980s, when women finally felt secure in the workforce, we experienced an abundance of brightly colored suits and dresses being worn to the office. In 1992, when the fashion industry tried to put women back into men's apparel, the concept was totally rejected by these consumers. It seems that consumers are telling us that color creates or at least expresses their moods.

Menswear has also experienced more and more color in apparel and furnishings, starting with casualwear and active sportswear. Color then moved into knitwear, and most recently we are beginning to see brightly colored sports jackets.

In the home furnishings market, we are also experiencing more use of color. People have discovered that certain colors create different moods. For example, a room with soft coral walls creates a glow on everyone's skin tone and seems to have a calming effect on everyone present. Bright colors used in the kitchen, at the dining table, or at pool side create a happy effect.

As I work on the next season's colors, I have always considered what I have projected the season before. Colors evolve gently from one season to the next. It is very important to study consumer response to certain color families and then work through those families to the next level. For example, if red is selling well at retail and has peaked, then I would move toward a more rosy tone or a coral, depending on what I had projected before red.

When I am developing color, I consider all aspects of the world at large. I study whether the economy is doing well or not. I analyze spending habits and what people are doing with their money. Obviously, if people are deeply concerned about their future and whether or not their job is secure, they will not buy items in dusty or dirty tones. They will tend to respond to colors that are more upbeat. I also consider where people are going on vacations and what they are doing on those vacations. What are they doing in their free time? Are they practicing physical fitness? Are they gardening? Are they cooking? What are their concerns? Are they into saving our planet? If so, obviously greens and blues are important.

Other factors influencing my color projections include whether or not people act aggressively toward one another. The 1980s were full of aggressive jobs and attitudes; until "Black Monday" it seemed as if that spirit would never end. But it did, and with it evolved a kinder, more peaceful attitude in our dealings with one another, which has resulted in softer, gentler color feelings.

Today, people are becoming more tolerant of each other's ethnic backgrounds, realizing that there is something unique in each ethnic culture. As the fashion pendulum swings from one culture to another, those cultures also influence the business of projecting color.

In addition, I consider the impact of art and various influential exhibitions, music trends, and rock stars. Last of all, I watch what the influential designers show in their collections in Paris, Milan, London, and New York. And I pay careful attention to what is happening in Los Angeles and New York.

Because my client base is so diverse—ranging from fabric mills to manufacturers of all types of apparel and accessories, leather tanneries, shoe and handbag manufacturers, bed and bath mills, cosmetic and hair care companies, paint companies and automobile producers—all must be considered when I project colors for the next season.

The most important thing to realize is that color is the first visual impression the eye registers, whatever it focuses on. Color is everything.

Shopping Is In-Depth Market Research
Kay Stephenson Wrack

157. *The constant colors. Courtesy of Kay Stephenson Wrack.*

Color forecasting more than blind faith is a major marketing tool or product delineator, and is profitable if done right. In my own color work, I look at everything, then I look for the missing colors.

Color Counts

Looking, tasting, smelling, hearing, and touching are my color research, in order to be exquisitely aware of trends and nuances, of the major movements and minutia that drive our culture, and, thus, our markets.

Homework? Research? Information omnivore! I look at everything: flea market finds, haute couture, other people's color forecasts, four newspapers a day, reproachful stacks of magazines waiting to be opened, the morning news, and supermarket tabloids. How are we doing? Are we earning less or spending more? Saving? Being saved? Losing Money? Feeling blue? In the pink? Getting older, getting better? Anything and everything can and will influence color trends (fig. 157).

158. *Shopping is in-depth color research. Courtesy of Kay Stephenson Wrack.*

Shopping Is In-Depth Market Research

Things that I think about, look at, and consider include: street smarts, the counter-culture, Harleys and "pigs" (they're black except when they're Japanese and kid's clothes bright). Do mica fleck fenders segue into frosted eyeshadow? And do the boomers control all? Maybe. It's all out there, and I'm looking.

Looking/shopping . . . we've gone beyond canned peas, they have to be fresh and so very green. Peppers, the beginnings of a nascient rainbow in green, sunny yellow, truly red, and now in glossy purple. T-shirts, once they were white; now they sell in high-fashion hues and PC black. Fifty percent of linens are sold in white, but the other fifty percent will leave the store in colors. Which colors? My research, my job (fig. 158).

Am I futurist or a forecaster? Why color? I research eclectically and in depth; scientific breakthroughs, government legislation, demographic trends, sales by style. I ask questions. Is your favorite soap opera sending a color message? How will the growing importance of the

159. *Food fashion forecast. Courtesy of Kay Stephenson Wrack.*

Asian, Hispanic, and immigrant consumers impact on color? Does cost count, and will we compromise our fashion and color expectations if the price is right? My findings and feelings could as easily be expressed as a spreadsheet, a bar graph, or a pie chart. I chose color.

Some Things Never Change

The constant colors, the colors of our culture: red, white, blue, camel, navy, burgundy, forest green, and black. Every spring, fashion rediscovers the fresh charms of navy and white, every autumn finds us delighting in russets and reds, plaids, and tartans. Every man's mufti: navy blazer, grey slacks, and a bright red tie. A red sports car, red lollipops, and why is Revlon's perennial best-selling lipstick "Cherries in the Snow"? In our rough and tumble world of brave new families and financial fluidity we need constants and continuity (fig. 159).

Sophisticated, worldly, dashing, dowdy. Will we ever go beyond black? We no longer mourn, yet

160. *Yet another look at neutrals. Courtesy of Kay Stephenson Wrack.*

dress to be ready. Why do we persist in black? In our dishes, our cars, our clothes, we've seen a gold-chained diaper bag in black. Is this black despair a defense, whistling in the dark, braving the re-surgence of disease and starvation? Or is black worldly sophistication? A cloak of safety in cities of no eye contact . . . or will it lead to a spring time of color?

Keep Watching!

Food as color barometer. How we eat, what we eat, where we eat. When we are munching granola and seven grain breads, our desires tend towards unbleached white cottons, beige wool, and brown wood—the natural and perceived to be real (fig. 160).

But we eat fast foods, sit on RTA furniture, and work in the home office. Life in the fast lane. It may lead to brave new worlds but also to recycled colors and recycled styles. Yesterday's icons, yester-day's fashions, and the re-emergence of meatloaf, mashed potatoes, and yet another look at neutrals. Safe? Like being folded into Mommy's apron (fig. 161).

Not "safe": the Restaurant Temple and the Gourmand Bouffe, as structured as theater. The well-made plate, and the reviewer critiques the colors and decor before the dinner. Food as expression, plays of color: the flash of correct lettuce and today's greens, lashings of lemon, the pinky coral of roe and inky black risotto *nero*. Who decides the culinary colors, the palate? This is the domain of the super chef; the eagerly sought

161. *The persistence of black. Courtesy of Kay Stephenson Wrack.*

seating in a setting as perfectly planned and balanced as the evening's culinary offering. The food and the decor compliment and balance. The bread, the banquet, the salad, the setting.

What Are We Doing and When Can We Stop?

Our fears, our thoughts, concerns about body and health, aging and AIDS, the sandwich generation. Are we healthy? Enough? Am I making the most of my body, should I be making a healthy choice? We're looking for comfort, reassurance, and safety.

How does this translate into market color? Will traditional colors of comfort re-emerge? Health care's well-conceived cheer? New whites of pristine purity? Fiesta Ware in nonlead brights? The cuddly greyed colors of fuzzy toys and flannel blankets, and low-calorie cocoa by a roaring fire?

Too busy to eat, too busy to shop . . . till we drop. A nation tuned to convenience, the "Bed in a Bag," "Bath in a Box," total coordination in all purchases, because "Who has time to shop?" The effect on color is predictable, and matched. Everything goes with everything. Consumer-proof coordinates. The triumph of forecasting, and color cards, and the mass market.

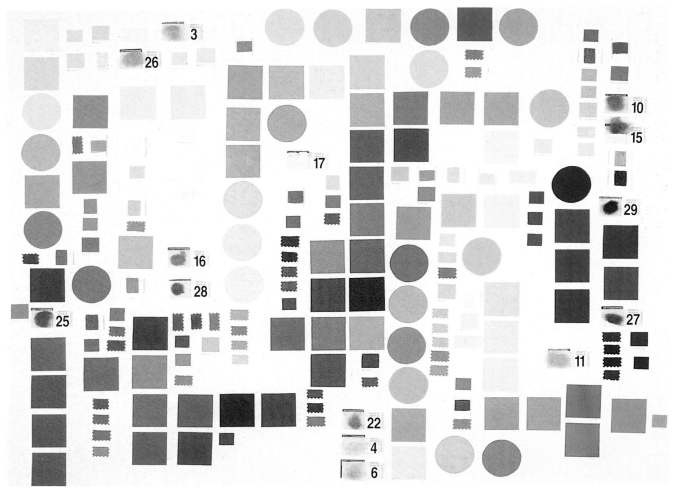

162. *Composite forecast board. Courtesy of Kay Stephenson Wrack.*

In my looking and my research I collect the color cards that industries and organizations so kindly prepare . . . the color forecast service cards too, fee for color. They all make color forecasts and I make chromatic composites. Occasionally, I have the uneasy feeling that everyone is reading the same magazines, attending the same shows, consulting the same sirens, feeding from the same table. Sameness and coordination are to the good of the market comfort and product coordination when millions of dollars ride on a single new introduction. Still, we're driven to look for the flash of newness, a color that will define, create desire, and drive purchases. The search keeps us aware, honest (figs. 162–163).

And Not to Forget:

All the worldly things and ideas and movements and events and people that will impact on color,

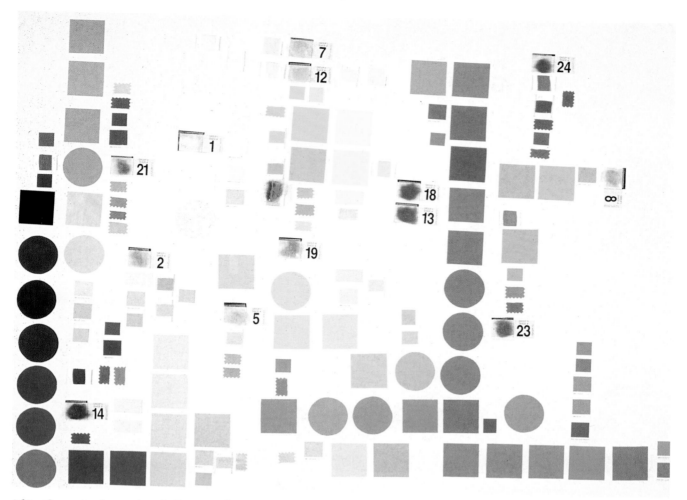

163. *Composite forecast board. Courtesy of Kay Stephenson Wrack.*

drive color, drive our markets. Ecology, baby boomers, empty nesters, new architecture, the global economy and global warming. Cowboys and Indian artifacts. Visible minorities and the underground economy. Who did it in the movies and what were they wearing? Promos and demos. Mall rats and street smarts. OSHA, TV, NRA, NOW, PC, AC/DC. The greying of America. The Green Revolution. Don't bungle the jungle. All of this and more become color forecasts, delight

designers, open markets, create desire, sell products, soothe the ill, reflect our dreams, and define our share of the world.

To forecast color, I look at everything, then I look for the colors that just feel right.

164. *"Fresco" presentation board used to demonstrate use of midtone-tinted jewels. Courtesy of Diane Calvert.*

Part Six
Notes on Fashion Color Forecasting

From French haute couture to American ready-to-wear, consumer color preferences in fashion have grown more sophisticated. Color has a central and complex role in its success because the demands for mixing, juxtaposing, and personalizing colors continues to grow. Layering colors and multiple combinations created on the computer are also providing fashion designers with new insights, techniques, and tools for color possibilities, as well as a means to respond quickly to market demands. In a multifaceted fashion industry, the manufacturers of belts, gloves, stockings, and hats play a dynamic role paralleling the clothing industry. With continuing exchange between the American, European, and Japanese fashion industries, color influences from around the world's fashion capitals mix cultural events, economics, politics, and psychological moods to reflect a myriad of design possibilities in our era.

Textile Design and Apparel

Diane Calvert

The seasonal color forecasting services, both European and American, are invaluable to me as a textile designer and color consultant. The Europeans tend to be sophisticated, with color ideas that are more subtle and difficult to understand initially; the Americans are more basic.

The use of any forecast requires professional interpretation and management from season to season. Although an exciting forecast can inspire the creative thinking of product developers and buyers, new color direction can also be confusing. A forecast may be a dramatic departure from previous seasons, or it may be a variation on a long-playing theme. There is always a risk of overreacting to a forecast. Ignoring forecasts or playing it too safe can lead to new merchandise that looks anything but new.

Approximately eighteen months prior to every season, color forecasters present palettes of approximately fifty colors each, broken down into ranges of neutrals, darks, brights, midtones, and pastels. Seasonal forecasts are based on the women's wear market, since women's wear uses the widest spectrum of color. Men's and children's wear is developed by scaling down the wider color palettes forecasted for women's wear, adding darks and neutrals for men, pastels and brights for children.

Using European forecasters for the leading edge in color and the Americans for what's new in the basics, I determine the primary color focus and general trend of the season. By comparing one forecaster to another, I then find the color undercurrents. For fall 1993, green was the undercurrent in one forecast. The yellows, golds, blues, greys, and browns all leaned toward greens in the color spectrum, while the warm colors of reds, oranges, and purples were hued so that they complemented the green-casted cools. That undercurrent was the natural sequel to the major blue/green story of the previous season.

Working with approximately 200 to 300 colors from four to six forecasting services, I develop a palette of five to six ranges. Each range has twelve to twenty colors. These are the 75 to 100 colors the retailer works with each season. Each range is wide enough to accommodate several in-store deliveries without repetition of the same color.

The esoterica of forecasted color must be translated into a language that excites and inspires the retailer if the colors are ever to be understood by the consumer. I create a palette of tailor-made color ranges on portable presentation boards (five to six each season) with removable color yarn poms. Each board has its own theme communicated with photographs and imagery to introduce the palette, and show how color can conjure up specific moods. The boards inspire product developers to think imaginatively about ways to use the forecasted colors in the upcoming season.

For example, I might communicate a range of midtone, tinted neutrals under the theme "Fresco" through a presentation board that evokes the centuries-old painted walls of Italian churches. I might also feature pictures of stone vaulting colored by the ages in hues of beige, mauve, and mossy grey. A range of "knockout" brights, such as ruby, amethyst, lapis, emerald, and gold, I might present as "Byzantine Jewels," with color imagery taken from illuminated manuscripts, mosaic columns and stained-glass windows (figs. 164–165). For the "Fresco" theme, I would include photographs of chunky, neutral-colored knits, classic yarn-dyed plaids, and simple but sophisticated prints; for "Byzantine Jewels," rich paisley patterns, silk jacquards, lush velours, and intricate, brightly colored prints.

Once the color palettes are established, I move the client into production with textile designs, fabric samples, and silhouettes of possible garments. (The forecasting services are useful in

165. *"Byzantine Jewels" presentation board used to demonstrate use of jewel-toned brights. Courtesy of Diane Calvert.*

this regard as their products suggest ways of using new colors in printed and yarn-dyed fabrics.) Finally, I refine the color range for each in-store delivery by designing myself, or guiding in the purchase of original print designs from design studios. Each projected garment is drawn in color with a full-sized croquis of the print or yarn-dyed pattern. The garment drawings and croquis are then put into story-boards as a permanent record of each in-store delivery for the season.

Several guidelines should be applied to any tailor-made palette. The first is to base the palette on the level of sophistication of the market. An upscale, trend-conscious market will want a palette more European in overall feeling, while a mass-market retailer will want a palette to be more understandable and approachable. New York City is viewed as more sophisticated; the midwest is more traditional. A sun belt or California consumer will usually favor primary brights over the more conservative neutrals of a colder climate.

Some markets have virtually unchanging tastes. The eastern penchant for preppie hunter greens, burgundies, and navies is an example. In such cases, that preference has to be adapted with new colors in the same range or with a similar mood or feeling, which makes the consumer feel comfortable while looking new enough to make her feel fashionable.

Second, if there are enough colors that the consumer is asking for year after year, I update those colors with a fresh look, or with new ideas for matching a long-favored color with something new and different. If jade has been a best-seller, I will include a jade with a new undertone of blue or yellow, depending on the seasonal forecast.

Colors can be put together in new combinations and ways that make them appear new. If an earlier season's colors were communicated through an equestrian theme, using classic tartans, hunting motifs, and the deep, rich but traditional colors evocative of the English gentry, I might update that idea for the next season by creating a "library" theme featuring new forecasted tones of burgundy, navy, and hunter green shown through photos and samples of Persian carpets, leather book bindings, and marquetry tabletops of semi-precious stones and woods.

Forecasters occasionally try to recast classic colors for the sake of newness. In doing so, they may introduce colors that are not as wearable as the classics they are trying to replace. Depending on the market, a retailer might be well advised to ignore a forecasted green or purple so dark that it appears black, and simply retain basic black, which is more understandable to the consumer.

Some colors can always be problems in certain markets. European color forecasters tend to highlight browns more so than the American forecasters. Although Europeans wear brown, Americans shy away from it, and therefore retailers are afraid of it. But if brown is a directional color, I encourage a retailer to feature it in some way, perhaps in a yarn-dyed check or plaid, or as a prominent color in a print that features colors more accessible to the consumer.

Forecasts cannot be relied upon exclusively.

Some colors, such as black, white, true red, navy, and ivory are so basic that they seldom appear in a forecast. These are colors that never die and must be featured in every seasonal color range.

Paris haute couture also dictates directional colors from time to time that do not appear in a forecast. I will suggest that a retailer use these colors in printed or yarn-dyed fabrics so the consumer can marry the new color with her old favorites in order to feel that her wardrobe is being updated without taking her out on a fashion or financial limb.

Finally, color runs in cycles, and we are at the end of several seasons of brights. They will continue, but will be less dominant than they have been in previous seasons. Some of a retailer's and the consumer's favorite brights may have to be gradually replaced by midtones that can be accessorized with the brights of the previous season to avoid the gap of leaping from one distinct palette to a totally different one. Although a forecast will never show an identical color from one season to the next, I will choose new colors with enough similarity to those of previous seasons to make a smooth transition possible.

The Color of Excitement—
The Excitement of Color!

Pauline Ashworth

"She wore a red dress with black pumps and matching purse. Her nails were a deep ruby color and she drove a sporty convertible."

Whenever we as consumers think of fashion items we undoubtedly describe their color first and style or design second. Compare this statement with a description of those purchases which are more functional in nature; when purchasing an automobile or kitchen appliances, for example, although the color choice is without question an influence on purchase behavior, that selection is frequently made after the initial brand selection process has been completed. Performance, function, and design are important, and color adds to the excitement.

In the case of fashion purchases, each season consumers wait to see the new colors and the way in which those colors are merchandised together to create a palette. Indeed, style, design, and fabrications are an issue, but a color palette that is not appealing to the audience will lose sales, regardless of the garment or product styling. Add to this the notion that fashion thrives on change and a clear picture of the challenge of fashion marketing is apparent.

As with any item, in fashion marketing we develop a strategy for positioning the product in the marketplace. The way in which the consumer perceives the product is, to all intents and purposes, reality. The brand image must be cohesive and must evolve seasonally without changing and risking the loss of the customer base. In many cases, this brand image can be highly defined in terms of color. A consumer will frequently gravitate and demonstrate loyalty to those brands that offer colors which she feels suit her, as long as the products themselves are suited to the function. In other words, the relationship is to an extent built on trust, the trust that this season's new looks will continue to satisfy the brand's loyal consumers by making them feel good.

The question then is how do we as fashion marketers move the brand forward in terms of color without turning off the audience? Where do fashion palettes come from and how quickly do they change?

The answer is in two parts; the first part addresses the issue of general color directions in fashion, and the second is the adaptation of those trends to a specific brand and, therefore, a specific consumer segment.

In establishing the general color directions,

forecasters will consider all factors that may influence color choices in a particular time frame. Fashion palettes evolve, and the speed at which they change must also be addressed. Each morning the consumer makes a color decision for that day, a decision invariably made on the basis of the relationship between color and mood. If the mood is somber, then the consumer may subconsciously wear only a selection of her wardrobe in a particular time frame, namely those colors that suit her mood. In forecasting fashion directions, this relationship between color and mood is the basis for the palette decision. For example, changes in the economy will influence fashion choices. During recessionary times, fashion purchases are frequently more neutral and more serious, and yet at the same time bright colors may represent the add-on purchase, the psychological lift, and, of course, a marketing opportunity.

Other factors for consideration would be lifestyle changes, which would affect the role of fashion in the consumer's mind. Social and cultural environments from the movies or art exhibits will in some form exert their influence. The role of the forecaster is to analyze these movements and to decide the extent to which they may influence the marketplace. From these considerations will evolve the color direction for the season. Currently, the general trend is toward slower change, as consumers have demonstrated that right now fashion is not a high-priority issue for them.

The second part of the development process is the selection of a specific palette for a defined market segment. Knowing the consumer is all-important; her lifestyle, her aspirations, and her fears play a key role. The first consideration is the brand image: what will our consumers expect to see this season? There must be a mix of excitement generated by change and the comfort of not making radical changes. Editing plays an important role in this second part, the editing of those general considerations that may not be relevant to this market segment. Those typical marketing mix factors such as geographical distribution of the product, competitive activity, and sales history will influence the final palette. Decision-making time means that all these factors must be condensed into a limited number of colors. The term *directions* is no longer appropriate when seasonal sales are at stake. The number of colors that can be used is limited. In cosmetics, for example, the whole marketplace must be served by sometimes as few as four colors for a seasonal color story. In other words, in spite of the philosophical thought process through which the color palette may be developed, the bottom line is that the excitement created by one or two colors must be strong enough to motivate purchase.

Peclers Paris
Irène Zessler

166. *Irene Zessler with PECLERS PARIS stylists team in color direction meeting. Courtesy of Irene Zessler, PECLERS PARIS.*

I've always been fascinated by the color in our lives, by its presence in the landscapes and in paintings, and how it translates into the decorative arts, textiles, and particularly, into clothing. I was trained as an artist, and I worked as a painter for a number of years. Having always been attracted to clothes, and specifically to fabrics (materials and textures), these impulses have come together for me in my profession as a designer. At PECLERS PARIS, I have primarily designed fabric collections, and have researched materials, graphics, and color ranges. Since the founding of the company in 1970, we have always created our own color range. This private range was designed for use within the office, and created a language for work and communication among the PECLERS PARIS stylists. It was used in all areas of the textile industry, for our spinning, weaving, manufacturing, and retail clients. This range was developed in a very artsy fashion. I myself looked for the ink colors—and then had them handpainted on large boards. Ultimately, the success and usefulness of this color range as office work tool led us to publish and sell it.

167. *PECLERS PARIS studio color library. Courtesy of Irene Zessler, PECLERS PARIS.*

How We Create the PECLERS PARIS Color Range

Publishing the color range has naturally altered our work methods. As a presentation, it now has a strict framework that requires a particular discipline: a certain number of colors, color combinations, and photos to illustrate each range, which are then placed within a specific context each season.

Seasonal publication dates are fixed far in advance in order to coincide with the Première Vision salon (for fall, mid-March; for spring, early October) and we must keep production and manufacturing deadlines in mind.[1] I begin to

work on colors approximately two years before they are actually bought and worn by the consumer. What guides me in the beginning, keeping in mind this strict framework, is subjectivity. I always begin by putting myself in the place of the consumer, and by spontaneously buying yarns, ribbons, fabrics, books, photos—whatever strikes my fancy.

Then, having amassed a treasure trove of various elements, fabrics, and images, I try to rationalize my quest. For that, I go to brainstorm sessions with other design offices, but mostly I organize work sessions among stylists at our own office, where each person brings his or her inspirations for fabrics and colors, as well as design ideas. We try through our instincts and knowledge of the market to sense fashion's forward evolution as it

---

1. *Première Vision:* fabric show that takes place in Paris twice a year, and where PECLERS PARIS has a stand. Besides, PECLERS PARIS also takes part in brainstorm sessions to define *Première Vision's* promotional colors—as well as *Expofil's* and the *Sehm's*.

168. *PECLERS PARIS studio color library close-up on swatches. Courtesy of Irene Zessler, PECLERS PARIS.*

keeps up with the important cultural and social trends, and to determine how that evolution will manifest itself through materials, fabrics, and colors.

PECLERS PARIS' color range is, first and foremost, a fashion range specifically designed for clothing fabrics. However, in the last few years we have noticed that objects in other sectors of our daily environment renew themselves faster than before, and that they are more and more influenced by fashion. Thus, it often happens that a color developed with a T-shirt or jacket in mind ends up as a knife handle or a comforter.

Of course, to put the finishing touches on the color range—and this is the biggest job—I must synthesize, organize, and range the colors, and choose those that we will keep and emphasize.

What helps me in my decision at that point, other than a reflection on past seasons and, as I mentioned previously, a definition of seasons to come, is my sense for the colors themselves, for the subtlety and value of each shade, and for the way in which they can be worked together throughout the season. How then can we translate this mass of colors into a viable work tool and then into grounds, so that clients can personalize it according to their need and their creativity? I think that having a good taste for color responds to a more profound, highly irrational need, which we try to predict, to arouse, and to orient by playing a game that is both free, yet at the same time restricted to an organized color palette (figs. 166–172).

169A. *Inks to prepare hand-painted colors. Courtesy of Irene Zessler, PECLERS PARIS.*

169B. *Inks to prepare hand-painted colors. Courtesy of Irene Zessler,
PECLERS PARIS.*

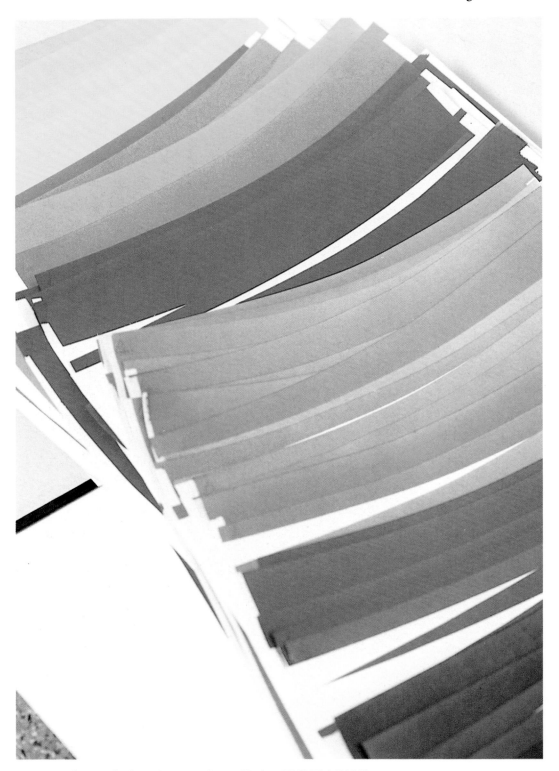

170. *Hand-painted colors. Courtesy of Irene Zessler, PECLERS PARIS.*

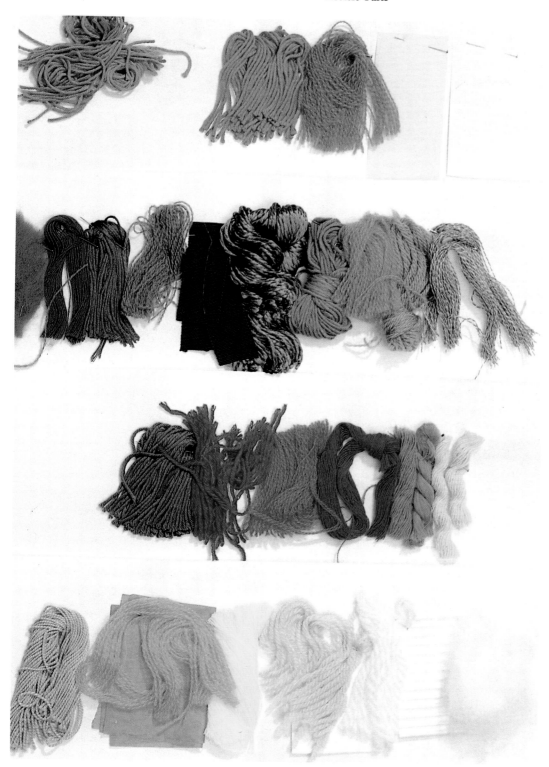

171. *Organization of colors in ranges before final printing. Courtesy of Irene Zessler, PECLERS PARIS.*

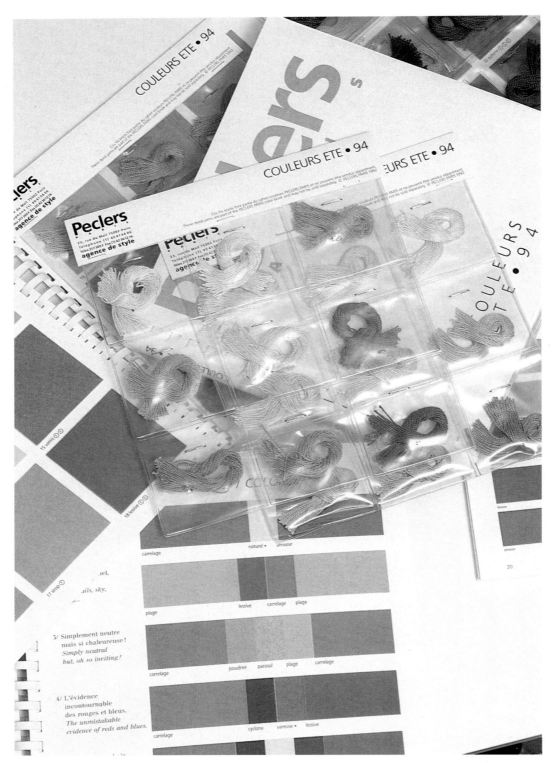

172. *PECLERS PARIS color card: the palette, the paper and yarn swatches, and the color combinations. Courtesy of Irene Zessler, PECLERS PARIS.*

Timing Is Everything
Alison L. Webb

I began forecasting colors in 1978 for a major fiber producer in the United States and, in more recent years, have been planning and forecasting colors for a large fabric manufacturer, several home fashion and accessory firms, and have done a variety of special projects for a diverse group of manufacturers whose products range from picture frames to biomedical equipment.

Much of my experience has been in the apparel and home fashions areas of the textile industry. It is unusual for a forecaster to work in both of these markets, but I find the similarities and differences between them very stimulating. I have just completed work on products for the spring 1994 apparel season—almost eighteen months ahead of the selling season. I am also developing colors for Home Fashions 1994 at about the same timing. Forecasting is always done very early, allowing for manufacturing schedules of fabric mills, clothing makers, and retail planning. My colors for spring 1994 were completely set in August of 1992— approximately twenty months in advance.

The Method

The methodology I use to approach a color palette for a forecast is pretty much the same in any business. It is essential to begin with a knowledge of the seasons prior to the one you are working on. A forecaster also thinks in terms of goods in the stores at a particular time of the year, keeping in mind the colors for the previous season. In a sense, I have cultivated the ability to plan with a historic visual sense or recall because colors evolve in a kind of "bell curve," typically over a three-year period.

For example, there are times when bright colors are very important in product lines. You know through research where these bright colors are in the market, when they first developed, and how they have evolved through the market. Did you have them last season or not? Were they saturated or thin? Were they based on primary colors or offbeat, unusual ones? How should they be developed for the next season?

It is also important in this business to develop a sense for timing. To me that means how will you introduce a brand-new group of colors? Or if they are not new, how will you make them somewhat different from the previous season and, therefore, new and exciting? A large measure of forecasting methodology is simply knowing where you have been and having a sense for the visual rhythm of color palettes as they work their way through the bell curve.

The European Connection

There is a long tradition and history of fashion creativity starting in Europe. It's not the only place of fashion creativity, but it is still a strong influence on our market. There are a number of reasons why this is so.

When you attend a week of European fashion shows—one show right after the other—you see a burst of creativity and many new ideas. It can be very directional for a color forecaster, as well as many other design professionals. European colors do have to be modified for the American market. Generally, Americans like their colors cleaner, brighter, and less complex—European colors tend to be darker, deeper, and more neutral based.

The aspect of fashion that makes it unique among industries is that it turns so quickly. The need for newness in color is like a monster's hunger that is never satiated. The need for color input in fashion is ongoing and constant. A great deal more color is generated by and comes out of the fashion markets than other markets. This is because major clothing manufacturers may help ship clothes into the stores every six weeks and need a new color feeling for every one of these clothing groups.

A Fix on the Market

Forecasters and designers from all over the world are continually trying to get a "fix" on what is

173. *Tracking color trends. Color board. Courtesy of Alison Webb.*

happening, which makes color design very interesting. Their sources of information can be what's happening in the current art scene (i.e., how color is being used in painting, graphic design, and creative publications, publications such as *Architectural Digest, French Vogue,* etc.) and what they see on television and at the movies. There is a communality of information shared around the globe now in a way that probably did not exist ten years ago.

At certain times, color in fashion gains its inspiration from other sources. For example, there has been an important retrospective of the artist Henri Matisse in New York. Because Matisse was both a colorful and decorative painter, this exhibit will influence the color palette. These cultural high points can't help but stir up the imagination, as do other high-energy moments in the allied disciplines of design, architecture—or wherever experimentation takes place in the arts.

Testing Ideas

When I begin to develop color for a client, I start with a visual concept by pinning up a group of colors that look good together—chosen from a basket of ideas from my own library, research files from Europe, and elsewhere. I continue to pin up groups of colors that look good to me, for example, darks that I want to look very flat like vegetable dyes—not terribly saturated, but subdued. Then I begin to edit, weed out, and adjust colors (figs. 173–174).

During this time, I am not paying great attention to what I discussed earlier about where color has been in the previous twenty months, but just studying relationships and colors in groups with a relatively open and free mind. I like to allow myself the opportunity to walk away from these initial studies and return to them—to look again, as part of the creative and assimilating

174. *Tracking color trends. Color board. Courtesy of Alison Webb.*

process. After this initial effort, I will go back to the previous season's work and edit the new range appropriately. It takes time to reach thoughtful decisions—and you never have as much time as you would like.

The Mass Market

In most cases, the mass market accepts new colors more slowly than the top end of the market. If bright colors first surface in the better market in one year, they won't be in the mass market until the next year. You plan a color palette so that it addresses those differences. Conversely, a number of mass-market companies take pride in quickly moving into new or fashion colors, particularly if they sell junior fashions.

Businesses never make color decisions based on one person's judgment alone. It's a consensus. People who rely on my forecast also obtain information and forecasts from other people like me. A consensus of opinions is gathered during the season, which eventually leads to color as the consumer sees it. Color forecasters help to focus opinion as well as express their own taste and point of view. Some companies work with several color forecasters, while others employ one individual.

Knowing thoroughly what market you're working for is very important to the forecaster—are you selling mass market, middle market, or are your products going to the high end? Also, the general business climate often has a great influence on what directions the palette takes. If business is slow or off, the market is more reluctant to change colors than when business is strong. When you color forecast for a fiber company, there are many different markets you have to cover (e.g., woven fabrics, knits, active wear, lingerie, sweaters, blouses).

Sharing Inspirations

Between the home and fashion industries that I am involved with daily, there is great cross-fertilization—one industry affecting the other. Home fashions colors generally follow apparel fashion colors. The reason for this relates in part to the quick nature of fashion. For example, during the last few years we have seen brighter colors in clothing at retail and a shift toward a warmer palette from the dominant cooler one of the 1980s.

These more saturated, warmer, yellow-based colors are beginning to make their way into home fashions. As people begin to see a color happening first in clothing, a shift to seeing it in the home becomes more acceptable. Conversely, especially today, many clothing designers also look to trends in furniture design, architecture, and the decorative arts as a rich source of inspiration. The feeding of color from industry to industry is a natural response to the rich sources of inspiration that surround us all.

Growing Into the Profession

There are many factors that contribute to becoming a color forecaster and being recognized in the field. Working for a number of years in the design and color industry obviously has a great deal to do with discovering your own abilities and talents. Typically, a forecaster's customers who work with their color ranges over a few seasons will find that these colors work well for their products.

Because businesses have a substantial investment in color decisions, they are going to get information from more than one source. Never-

theless, if three forecasters are putting forth bright red, a company may decide to use the particular red on my card versus the others. Because my color forecast is ready far ahead of the season, fabric mills rely on my information first, followed by apparel manufacturers. In this way, my color forecast influences all those businesses downstream from fiber production.

Related industries, such as shoes, accessories, and cosmetics, will also ask for the color forecast. Color forecasters are rarely radically different from each other—which is, perhaps, a phenomenon of nature unto itself. The Color Marketing Group people share color predictions after working up their individual forecasts independently. Time and time again, the palettes will be very similar.

Forecasters gain special awareness about color from working in particular industries. They discover aspects and problems of color related to their industry that are often unlike those of other industries. In this sense, we become specialized through experience and practice in the field.

Looking Ahead

In looking ahead, I feel that the 1990s are going to continue to be a colorful decade in both apparel and home fashions. I see clothing becoming more casual and comfortable and consumers giving a high priority to making their homes comfortable and cozy. The palette will be warmer overall than cooler, with less reliance on primary colors and safe neutrals and more interest in softer, more sophisticated colors. In general, the color intensity of the 1990s will be richer and colors will be complex.

The Japan Fashion Color Association
Bunta Idei

The Japan Fashion Color Association (JAFCA) is a Japanese group established in 1953 with the goal of conducting research relevant to fashion colors all over the world. Its vocation is to contribute to help develop industries and represent the culture of Japan. The results of JAFCA research are widely distributed throughout the country by the membership and a variety of sponsored meetings and color-forecasting activities. Over 1200 members represent such industrial and commercial companies as ladies's, men's and children's clothing as well as the related businesses of leather goods, jewelry, underclothing, stockings, and architecture, lighting, housewares, interior design, furniture, linens, schools, and universities.

Commercial activity is well represented by large retail chains and shops. Associate members create, publish, and disseminate information through leaflets, color card samples, research reports, and marketing inquiries. The monthly magazine *Ryuukoo Shoku* reflects a broad assortment of JAFCA activities and interests in color, as well as listings of special papers and other periodicals available. Although it is published in Japanese, there are numerous sponsored color studies created that would be of interest to an international audience, including:

- *JAFCA Basic Color Code*
- *Handbook for the Harmony of Colors*
- *Dictionary of Colors*
- *Fashion Color Trends*

Various special survey commissions are organized by the associate members regarding forecasts on many industries in Japan, and in coordination with appropriate public ministries, federations, and organizations in the field. JAFCA has been a member of INTERCOLOR group since 1963— the year of the foundation of that organization (figs. 175–177).

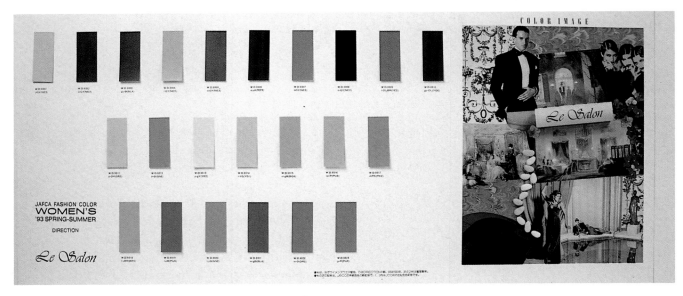

175. *Seasonal Color Cards for Women's Wear. Courtesy of JAFCA.*

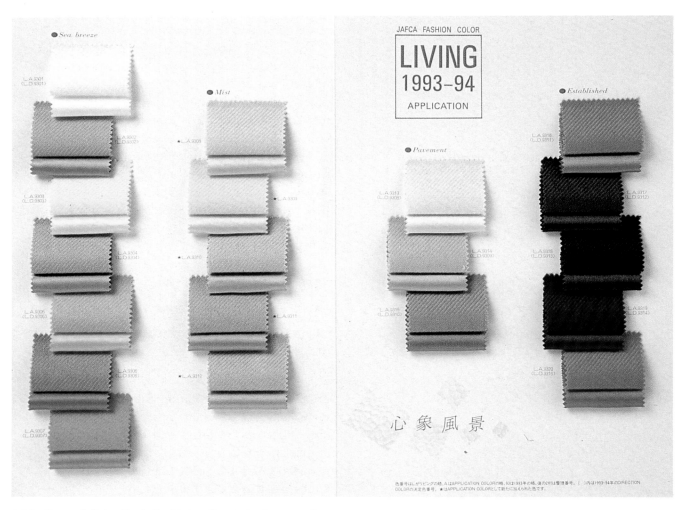

176. *Seasonal Color Cards for Living (Interior). Courtesy of JAFCA.*

平成4年1月1日発行　毎月1回1日発行　昭和36年11月22日　第三種郵便物認可

1992 No.418

流行色

1

JAFCA FASHION COLOR 92AWメンズ

177. *Monthly magazine,* Ryuukoo-shoku, *Fashion Color. Courtesy of JAFCA.*

178. *Cachet makes it surprisingly easy to turn an original scan into an image suitable for publication (below right). Cachet's MultiChoice option makes it easy to correct an image by choosing the alternative you like best (top and bottom center). Photo courtesy of Electronics for Imaging Inc.*

Part Seven
Technology and the Future

The digitization of color, along with continual advances in computer technology, will have the greatest importance for humanizing color imagery. Forecasting color for communications, design, and manufacturing industries with the computer will move from the mechanistic appearance to a greater dimension of visual experiences where complexity in color and human moods—natural textures and variety—are ultimately easily attainable. In the twenty-first century, the wholesomeness of color and technology, re-experienced in a new technological context and form, will redefine international design markets with new and unprecedented ranges of color experiences and directions.

The Dimensions of Color Experience[*]

Uri Feldman

For most people, color constitutes a routine aspect of everyday life. Color appears everywhere in such natural objects as flowers, fish, and rocks, and in such fabricated objects as athletic shoes, toothpaste, clothing, automobiles, soft drinks, and bubble gum. The use of color has been made even more widespread with the advent of computer-driven displays, which can show images with colors selected from a wide range of possibilities. However, even in such sophisticated display systems, color selection is usually based on the skill and memory of trained color specialists and designers, who in general treat colors as isolated visual phenomena.

In reality colors appear as interrelated visual sensations, unpredictable from looking at single colors in isolation. For instance, certain colors, when placed next to each other, can look exciting, as if vibrating at their boundaries. Others may look subdued when placed next to each other; still some other colors may look somewhere along a continuum between subdued and energetic. Thus, color experiences range between low magnitude and high magnitude. Experience of color is the response to color relationships, as determined by the magnitude of the interaction between colors.

It is proposed here that experience of color is universal. That is, humans make judgments about magnitude of interaction of colors based on how colors relate to each other. Features of the colors, such as chromatic composition and spatial configuration, determine the magnitude of the interaction. These features constitute the dimensions of color experience (Feldman, 1993).[1]

[*]Researches conducted by Uri Feldman reported in this article are exclusively his rights, Patent Pending.

1. Uri Feldman, "Quantifying the Dimensions of Color Experience," Ph.D. Thesis, Media Arts and Sciences Section, Massachusetts Institute of Technology, 1993.

Varieties of Experience

In visual communication, a wide variety of color experiences can be established. For example, figure 179A shows several patterns made up of two colors. Each pattern constitutes an experience of color; each has its own unique character. However, even among such varied experiences, it is possible to identify features that are common among the experiences: some energetic, some weak. Therefore, when evaluating color, what is most revealing is to determine how colors relate to each other. It is the relationship between colors that determines magnitude of experience.

For instance, the patterns in figure 179A can be organized by magnitude of experience. There is also a visually fluid passage of color experience demonstrated (fig. 179B).

The patterns in figure 179B have been arranged so that the least energetic patterns are near the bottom-left corner; the most energetic patterns are on the upper-right corner; all other patterns are somewhere in between. The transformations of experience along each of the sides of the square are established by traversing a different dimension of color experience. For instance, in figure 179B, the bottom segment shows a transformation along the dimension of hue contrast, where, from left to right, hues are getting farther apart from each other. The vertical segment on the left shows a transformation along the dimension of chroma or saturation, whereas, from bottom to top, chroma is increasing.

The dimensions of color experience provide the framework for establishing many visual sensations because they indicate how experiences relate to each other. The arrangement of patterns in a closed square loop suggests that experience of color transcends chromatic composition or spatial configuration. A given experience can be approached by following paths along different

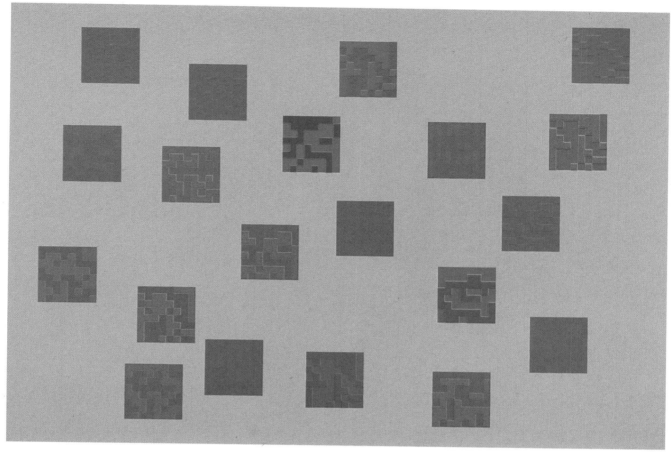

179A. *Varieties of experience. ©Massachusetts Institute of Technology. Courtesy of Uri Feldman.*

dimensions of experience, independent of which colors are chosen. For instance, energetic experiences can be produced around colors such as pink, which are not ordinarily considered energetic. When placed against a saturated olive or dark yellow-green, pink is seen as robust and energetic. Therefore, establishing experience of color becomes a matter of adjusting color relationships.

Establishing Experience of Color in Applications

In practice, treating colors as they are experienced can be used to provide answers to such questions as: "What information are color experiences providing?", "Can color experiences enhance the information being displayed?", "How do experiences relate to each other?", and "Can color experiences be predicted?"

The general approach for establishing color experience is to determine the color intent of the application.[3] The color intent determines the visual relationships required by the application. In this discussion, *application* refers to any situation that utilizes color as a way of conveying a message, such as graphic design, computer graphics, painting, display design, textile manufacturing, advertising, cinematography, etc.

2. William Cowan, "Color Selection for User Interfaces," Siggraph Course no. 10, Notes, ACM Siggraph, Boston, 1989.

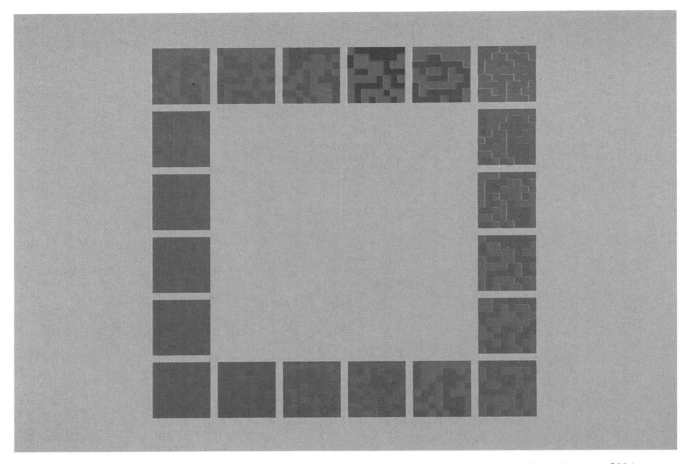

179B. *Varieties of experience arranged by magnitude of experience. ©Massachusetts Institute of Technology. Courtesy of Uri Feldman.*

Prototypical Experiences

Experiences corresponding to specific visual relationships are referred to as prototypical experiences. For example, in graphic design, if the intent is to highlight or draw attention to a feature, then a high-magnitude prototypical experience is required.[4] Such high-magnitude experiences can be established by selecting colors with high saturation or colors with large-hue contrast.

Thus, correspondence between task and prototypical experience must be established. In terms of color experience, the choice of prototypical experience amounts to selecting a magnitude of interaction that corresponds to the prototypical experience.

Transposing the Experience

If the intent of the application is to preserve the experience, then magnitude of experience is maintained. If, on the other hand, the intent is to transpose the experience, then magnitude of experience is varied by adjusting the contribution of each dimension to the overall interaction.

---

3. Nathaniel Jacobson, Walter Bender, and Uri Feldman, "Alignment and Amplification as Determinants of Expressive Color," Proceedings SPIE: Human Vision, Visual Processing, and Digital Display II, Vol. 1453, San Jose, February 1991.

What Experience of Color Is Not

When evaluating experience of color, agreement between people is large, meaning judgments of magnitude of experience constitute an invariant aspect of human response to color. Beyond such invariant response lie more personal and subjective issues of judgment, such as whether an experience is pleasant or not. The problem with assessing personal preferences is that there is no consensus among people, even less across people in different cultures, as to which colors are beautiful or ugly together. Therefore, subjective evaluation of color is different from how color is experienced.

Beyond Experience of Color

The dimensions of color experience allow for experiences to be adjusted with precision. Establishing experience of color can be guided by systematic compositional guidelines. The concepts presented here provide the framework for subsequent research in the field.

Cachet: Color for the Rest of Us*

Thad McIlroy

Cachet, a new Macintosh color enhancement and separation program from Electronics for Imaging (EFI), is the most important piece of desktop publishing software to hit the market since Aldus's PageMaker®. It makes getting high-quality color a simple proposition, even for those who don't have color prepress expertise.

To appreciate Cachet, it's important to make a distinction between color digital design and color digital prepress production. Currently, Adobe Photoshop® is the best-known, and by far the best-selling, program for desktop color. But Photoshop is primarily a design and painting program, with its role as a production tool playing second fiddle. Using Photoshop solely as a design tool is delightful, but its complex operation has kept quality prepress work a task strictly suited to color professionals.

Cachet, on the other hand, is dedicated solely to production. Its role is to correct scans for problems of lighting or exposure and to enhance their color appearance. It also saves the corrected scans in files that give the best possible results on your particular color printer or separates them for your production techniques.

Cachet's documentation promises that using the program requires no knowledge of color theory or color reproduction. EFI claims you need only visual skills: an appreciation of color and the ability to compare colors in two images. Initially, I was skeptical about Cachet's capability to come through on those promises, but after using the program, I was convinced.

By Reference Only

Many people assume that the purpose of color scanning and separation is the exact duplication of original artwork and photographs. In fact, this is rarely the case. Instead, color scanning and separation are dedicated to making originals look their best when printed on paper, compensating both for the flaws of the original and the limitations of the reproduction process. In other words, the true goal is adapting originals to the requirements of a specific publication.

Color correction tools adjust hue, saturation, brightness, and contrast. On top of that, creating four-color film separations involves understanding the effects of undercolor removal (UCR), grey-component replacement (GCR), halftone dot shapes, and screen angles. Not surprisingly, the average person rarely masters all these techniques. Photoshop provides most of the required controls for prepress production, but offers no simple process to master them. This is where Cachet so breathtakingly succeeds.

Cachet's two most important tools, Edit by Reference and MultiChoice, seem designed for the young at heart. They're fun to play with and straightforward to use.

Edit by Reference is based on the premise that if you compare your scan with one that has already been successfully corrected and printed, you can succeed through imitation. Cachet comes with 24 reference images, available both on disk and in a book printed on coated stock with a 150-line screen.

Your first task is to choose the printed reference image that looks the way you want your original, or working, image to appear when printed. The reference images offer a wide range of choices, including combinations of people with different skin colors, various lighting conditions, close-ups and long shots, country landscapes and city skylines, and several still lifes.

Once you've selected your reference image from the manual, you display that image's digital version on your monitor alongside your working image. Then you manipulate your working image until it looks like the reference image. When the two images are closely matched on screen, you can assume that your printed image will look the same as the printed version of the reference image. This approach eliminates most of the concern about monitor calibration, since you're matching two

*Reprinted by permission of *Publish*.

images on the same monitor, not trying to achieve a perfect display (fig. 178).

Multiple-Choice Color Correction

The easiest way to manipulate your image is using Cachet's MultiChoice tool within the program's ten control areas. When you want to correct the exposure of your scan, for instance, MultiChoice automatically displays six variations on your image (you can control the degree cf variation). You choose the one that you feel wins the most improved prize. Cachet then offers six new choices. When you no longer see improvement, you move on to the next area of concern, such as white-point adjustment.

Although the MultiChoice tool is always available to guide you, the program still demands that you use some judgment; otherwise, you might unknowingly correct an image to the point that your printer won't be able to reproduce it. You could, for example, make adjustments that cause clipping, which forces highlight and shadow areas into pure white or pure black. The program warns you of this problem, and the well-written user manual offers clear directions for solving it. When problems like this occur, however, image correction suddenly appears more complicated.

This brings us to the other face of Cachet. Behind the program's simple tools lie the concepts and vocabulary of traditional color prepress: white point, midtones, highlights, color cast, and saturation. You'll find yourself making complex color adjustments, while perhaps being only dimly aware of the significance of your actions.

As you are working through *Learning Cachet* and *Using Cachet,* the documentation supplied with the program, you will encounter many of the color production concepts that permeate high-end color production systems. The genius of Cachet is that small doses of color theory can become very effective when offered with such intuitive tools (fig. 178, top and bottom center).

Color and Consistency

The EfiColor® color management system, EFI's tribute to device-independent color, is integral to Cachet and its success. EfiColor automates the process of matching color among different devices, including monitors, printers, and imagesetters. It characterizes a variety of digital printers, as well as traditional offset printing processes, and offers a reasonable guarantee that corrections you make on your monitor will show up in printed output.

EFI's color scientists have cataloged the features of each device or process and built transformations into Cachet that take the idiosyncrasies into account. EfiColor makes dramatic improvements in the color-proofing capabilities of even modest technologies such as thermal transfer and dye sublimation.

Best of all, EfiColor operates automatically. When it's time to separate or print your Cachet-corrected files, just specify the output device, and EfiColor's device profiles handle the rest. You can also save a corrected file as RGB TIFF, CMYK TIFF, or DCS (four CMYK files and a PICT preview). These last two file formats include the EfiColor transformations for the printer you specify, so you can import your corrected image into another program and still get the benefits of Cachet. The program also enables you to export a JPEG-compressed version of your file.

As I said, I was skeptical at first, but I found the quality of the color work done with Cachet to be exceptional. I ran nine test files through the program; five of them were difficult scans that I had already reworked with Photoshop. In every case, I significantly improved their appearance using Cachet. I've also spoken to two color prepress professionals in New York and Los Angeles who consider Cachet's quality acceptable for their everyday work.

Precision Color on Desktop Systems*

Richard Herbert

Color monitors, color-capable application software, and color printers have recently entered the marketplace, offering users myriad ways to produce color documents.

While it is possible with these devices to create pleasant-looking documents and graphics, it has been extremely difficult—if not impossible—to ensure that the colors specified on screen will be the colors printed on the page. Furthermore, the colors appearing on the page are a challenge for commercial printers to replicate because there is no standard way to specify those colors.

The obvious solution to these color coordination problems is the solution found years ago by commercial publishers: adoption of a color standard. Thus, currently we are seeing a movement to align desktop publishing with the Pantone Matching System, and more recently the PANTONE Process Color System (fig. 180).

Of course, the elements of a desktop publishing system are different from those of the traditional color design and production systems. To effectively conceptualize, specify, and communicate color in a desktop publishing system, various media must be manipulated: (1) RGB monitors, (2) color proofing printers, (3) laser imagesetters, (4) prepress proofs, and (5) process color or spot color printing.

A variety of schemes have merged through which these different elements are coordinated with each other and with the Pantone Matching System.

RGB is a very ambiguous term. The red, green, and blue phosphors used to create color displays are different for each brand of display monitor. To define a Pantone color in terms of RGB constrains accurate display of that color only to the monitor on which it was matched, and at a specific white balance color temperature. To solve this problem so that Pantone colors can be viewed with a higher degree of accuracy than has been the case, colors must be defined by a device-independent method.

Pantone and Radius have settled on a method known as CIE (Commission Internationale de l'Eclairage). The CIE system, based on extensive experimentation with human color perception, is an internationally accepted method for objective color measurement.

Although the system can be represented in many different ways, Radius and Pantone have structured their definitions around chromaticity coordinates (x, yY) for two light sources: D50, the standard graphic arts illuminant, and D65, a popular daylight illuminant.

By defining both the chromaticity of Pantone colors as well as the chromaticity of the phosphors used in each particular monitor, it is possible to calculate the proper magnitude of the red, green, and blue values for each Pantone color, for each defined monitor without custom-matching on a color-by-color basis (fig. 181).

When used in conjunction with the Radius PrecisionColor Calibrator, this CIE-to-RGB calculation is brought to another degree of accuracy. By calibrating a monitor, a correction

*Reprinted from *Graphic Arts Monthly*, April 1991, © 1991 by Cahners Publishing Company.

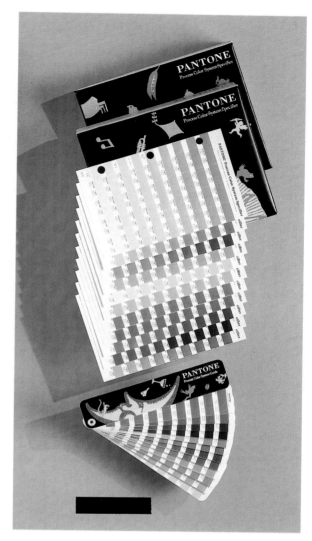

factor can be applied to the existing calculated data. This correction factor compensates for gamma (i.e., the nonlinearity in the light output of the monitor), as well as phosphor, decay.

Additionally, the white balance can be adjusted to the standard graphic arts illuminance D50, which has a white balance color temperature of 5000 K from its initial white balance setup. Hence, the white screen on the monitor looks more like a press sheet illuminated in a printing plant.

Identifying the monitor's characteristics and then controlling or adjusting for any variations from a preset standard allows Pantone colors to be displayed and controlled on these RGB devices. This means that the design and page layout process can be performed with a more realistic feel for how the finished piece will look.

180. *PANTONE Process Color System Specifier/Guide. Courtesy of Pantone, Inc.*

Pantone has custom-matched its colors to a selection of licensed hard copy output devices, including QMS Color Script 100, Oce Graphics G5232, NEC Colormate PS, Tektronix Phaser PX, and Seiko ColorPoint. A color lookup table is created at Pantone for each printer, consisting of percentages of yellow, magenta, cyan, and black (YMCK) for each Pantone color.

Millions of colors can be simulated with process color printing as employed by these computer printers. The number of colors varies with the screen ruling and the resolution of the device generating the halftones (fig. 182).

An example of the number of colors possible using the QMS ColorScript® printer is calculated as follows: 300 dpi halftone printer; 50 lpi screen

181. *Color monitor with PANTONE Color Palette. Courtesy of Pantone, Inc.*

ruling (comp quality); halftone cell size = 300/5 = 6; number of tints of any one color (6 × 6) + 1 = 37; and the total number of colors printable with process printing = 37^3 = 50,653 colors.

The broad spectrum of colors available on an inexpensive desktop output device, combined with its correlation to the Pantone Matching System, makes the thermal transfer printer a valuable comping tool for designers and graphic artists wishing their output to be an accurate link to the commercial press specifications on which they will rely for their final work.

Pantone has developed 150-line process color simulation data for each Pantone color for laser imagesetters. If the imagesetter can control its dot densities, these data will produce film that will enable four-color process versions of Pantone colors as visually demonstrated in the Pantone Process Color Simulator®.

Our company currently has two licensees in this area: the 3M Color Key and Polaroid Graphic

Imaging's Spectra Proof. The Color Key is available in a small selection of Pantone colors, while Spectra Proof simulates Pantone colors in both four-color process, as well as solid colors for the hard-to-get hues.

Other prepress proofing systems will provide accurate representations of the final printed piece if their toners adhere to Specifications for Web Offset Publications standards, and they can accept actual printing stock. An example of this type would be Kodak Signature. Iris ink-jet, and DuPont Cromalin and 4Cast systems are not acceptable methods for critical color matching and control because of the substrates used and/or the primary colors used.

Pantone provides color reference manuals that display thousands of color effects, from spot color to duotones to color and black to tints of Pantone colors and process color combinations.

Desktop publishing systems are usually configured with products from a variety of

182. *Color thermal transfer. Courtesy of Pantone, Inc.*

manufacturers. A typical professional-level desktop publishing system might include an Apple Macintosh computer, a Radius high-resolution color monitor, a Radius PrecisionColor Calibrator, software from Adobe and Quark, and a color proofing printer from QMS.

Because each product is developed by a different company, variances in the way colors are handled by these products can result in poor color compatibility and accuracy. Thus, a major factor in color calibration and control is the software component that can overcome these differences.

Radius and Pantone have worked together to provide a software package bridging the gap between the various products. This package, the Pantone ColorToolkit, provides a standard method for all licensees to implement colors on the Macintosh.

Until recently, professional graphic artists, designers, and production professionals have been reluctant to embrace desktop publishing technology because they were wary of inaccurate and unacceptable color results. The added uncertainty, the necessity of approximating, guessing, and double-checking color specifications, and the various stages of correction all served to compromise the cost and time savings for which desktop publishing methods are touted.

Now that software and hardware vendors are working together with Pantone to incorporate its system in all their various products, a level of color consistency is being achieved that stretches from the lowest-end desktop publishing system to the largest commercial press. The benefits will accrue industry-wide as inexpensive methods can be used to produce accurate comps and proofs, and commercial presses can rely upon specs provided by desktop publishing systems, instead of having to derive them anew.

Forecasting Color in the Graphic Arts Industry

Barry Ridge

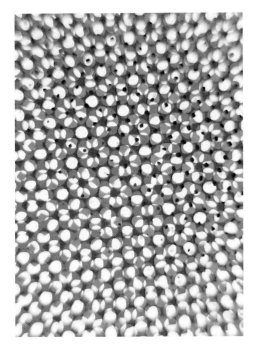

183. *Four-color process enlarged. The primaries create the secondary colors: yellow + cyan = green/yellow + magenta = orange/cyan + magenta = purple. Photo courtesy of Barry Ridge Graphic Design.*

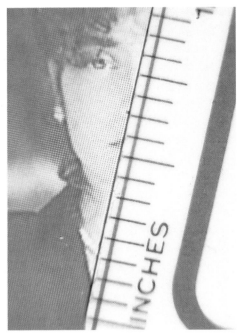

184. *Line screen includes a given number of dots per inch. The higher the line screen, the finer the resolution. Courtesy of Barry Ridge Graphic Design.*

The Digital Revolution

Forecasting color in the graphic arts industry is a matter of understanding the target audience and the expected longevity of the particular type of piece being produced. Being able to communicate effectively to that audience, through the very primitive subconscious level that color addresses is where art, science, and magic come together in one glorious blend of feeling. Does it, or does it not, feel right? Who is to say? Unfortunately, all we really have is the track record of sales. Does it or does it not sell? This is the measure that every forecaster of color must live up to. Understanding Process printing is a fundamental responsibility of every graphic designer and any marketing manager who expects to achieve any kind of satisfactory results in the reproduction of printed material (figs. 183–187). The last three years have brought about a complete metamorphosis within one of the largest industries in the country—the graphic arts.

The digital revolution in the graphic arts process will affect everyone who buys, sells, or creates anything for this huge industry. Communication through graphics touches everyone, print advertising, packaging, newspaper, video transmission, from manufacturer to consumer. The power of the printed message is still the most effective tool for marketing a product.

Similar to the industrial revolution of the 1880s and 1890s, the digital revolution of today is working its way into the lives of the average production person. Graphic communication is becoming one of the widest bridges, putting the results of this technology into the hands of the consumer. The challenges faced by everyone in the design community are numerous enough without having to relearn the most fundamental of tasks. Frustration is part of the learning curve. After those basic barriers are broken, creativity will begin

185. *This illustration shows finding the process equivalent of a solid forecast color in the* Process Tint Guide, *a printed reference that shows the palette of colors that can be created when different percentages of process color are overlaid with each other. Courtesy of Barry Ridge Graphic Design.*

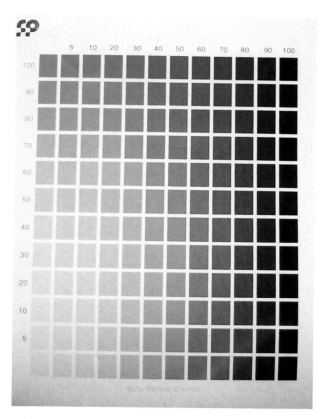

186. *As process density is increased a whole new range of colors is created. This illustration shows cyan and black with a 40-percent value of yellow. Courtesy of Barry Ridge Graphic Design.*

to come back with a whole new set of parameters. The days of fumbling through the process are over.

Preparing a project digitally for process printing must be planned and worked out from the inception of the job. A simple miscalculation on day one can be a monumental disaster when the work gets to the finishing stages of production (fig. 188). Today, the need for more and more technical knowledge and logical understanding is a necessity rather than just a nice addition to your resumé. Troubleshooting a system error is now part of a competent graphic designer's job description. When state-of-the-art becomes antique within three years, just how much change and adaptation can you absorb? The choices are endless. Anyone who has experienced a hard-drive crash, a corrupted EPS file, or a document that just won't run through the RIP of the film output device knows what I'm talking about.

Conventional Versus Digital

This is a term that you will be hearing again and again. To graphic arts professionals, it simply defines the old way from the new way. Whether you are directly involved with graphic arts by producing it or peripherally involved by purchasing graphic services, knowing the new terminology, software, hardware, and understanding the critical path of production is going to be mandatory if one wishes to continue to be involved.

Prepress

Prepress has always been a mystery to even the most experienced print buyer. Now that phase of production can be controlled by the designer, on screen from the initial setup of the job. Quantum leaps in reproducing accurate color for prepress proofing allow for a preliminary look at where the job is going, before expensive film and laminated

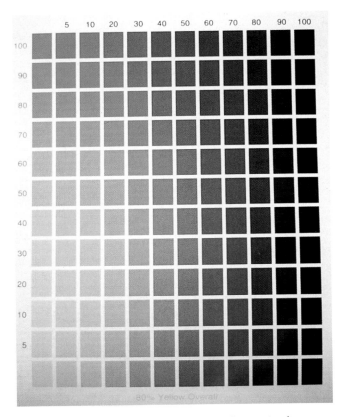

187. *Increasing the density further. This illustration shows cyan and black with an 80-percent value of yellow. Courtesy of Barry Ridge Graphic Design.*

188. *Controlling the sharpness of the dot is everything. The digital revolution in graphic arts is improving the accuracy in print production with more and more control for the designer. Courtesy of Barry Ridge Graphic Design.*

proofs are made. Digitized full-color imagery is becoming commonplace and affordable: The options for application of digital file are continually expanding; new methods in proofing using a color copier, color fax machines, color printing, oversized outdoor applications, conversion back to continuous tone, and multimedia presentations are all available.

Some of the claims being made by software and hardware manufacturers are overly simplified and sound a little too good to be true. There are certainly many pitfalls awaiting the user along the path of digital communications, but the possibilities of enhanced printed communications far outnumber the problems one will run into, while exploring this exciting new world.

Color in the Future
David Revere McFadden

Color is an integral element in the design process, defining and shaping our perceptions of space and volume. Even a brief glimpse at the history of the decorative arts confirms the power of color as the carrier of cultural messages; as a symbol of cultural, social, and familial indentity, color is primary in the traditions of heraldry and flag design, to cite two obvious examples. While color in such contexts connotes unity, color has also been used to provide immediate and visual confirmation of differences in status and class among people: Royal purple was limited in use to only the upper echelons of society.

While color has played a powerful role in all of the arts of design, it has been in the past two centuries that our understanding of the power of color has changed, primarily due to technological innovations. In the nineteenth century, natural dyes and pigments were replaced by synthetic chemicals that offered brilliant and long-lasting hues. The introduction of modern coloring agents radically changed the history of interior design, in that rare and often spectacular colors became available to a wider audience than ever before thought possible—to the delight of the manufacturing and retail sector. Hence, richly upholstered furniture, walls and carpets, window hangings and personal dress reflected this new world of manufactured industrial color. Printing technology likewise changed, offering brilliantly colored illustrations in popular books and magazines. And our perceptions of color itself were revolutionized as in systems of illumination,

beginning with gas and culminating in electricity, changed interior lighting and color dramatically and irrevocably. Whereas strong and brilliant colors were desirable for interiors lighted with candles, a new world of color stridences and subtleties was revealed in the glare of the electric light bulb.

The dramatic changes in the use and understanding of color that occurred in the nineteenth and early twentieth centuries has continued unabated. Now, with computer and laser technologies entering the daily routines of more and more people's lives, the potential for the use and exploitation of color are virtually limitless. These developments offer the greatest potential and challenges for designers today.

As we near the end of the twentieth century, we may be approaching the next major change in the use of color as a component of daily life. Color technology as it relates to private and public interior design has enormous potential in the next century (and the approaching millennium) as it is explored by industrial and interior designers, environmental professionals, and architects. New ways of manipulating color to alter our environments and our perceptions of space will be supported by continuing research on the effects of color on many aspects of our lives.

Much research has been conducted on the psychological and emotional impact of color on the quality of our lives, and certain proponents of alternative medicine posit beneficial effects that can be achieved in color therapy, effects that encompass the needs and deficits of mind as well as body. We are at the frontier of understanding the power of control to shape our experiences, our memories, and our attitudes. With the growth in medical technology, color and light may be used for home treatment of a variety of physical and mental needs, as well as to achieve the most restful and restorative environments, leisure, relaxation, and work. Possibly the use of color—achieved or revealed through innovative lighting technologies—may contribute to the healing arts at the broadest and most humane level.

Developments in understanding and using color as an integral element in the process of design will be informed by the growing body of knowledge being developed in other fields of expertise and specialization. This will require designers to reflect a more profound and holistic understanding of the potential of color. Rather than operating as an independent agent, tomorrow's interior designer will more likely work as part of an extended team of experts that may include environmental designers, computer programmers, and laser technicians. Alongside traditional ergonomic engineers and materials and manufacturing experts, this working group will be able to respond to the needs of universal design, which assures the highest integrity, functionality, and quality of design to the largest possible number of users and consumers.

The astonishingly rapid and seemingly limitless growth in electronic tooling available to the individual will undoubtedly continue to influence lighting technology and, hence, the use of color and light in the home and office, as well as in public spaces. While manufacturing theory and practice to date have concentrated on standardization, a shift toward customization to meet individual needs is both timely and inevitable. How the needs of customization align with the growth in color technology is already suggested by way of computer matching of colors for interiors, wall and floor treatments, and fabric design. While technology will provide a flexible matrix for production, it is in the ability of electronics to respond quickly and efficiently that will make customization and individualization the bywords of the coming decades.

Color in the home, for example, may be manipulated by electronic sensors that interact with the outside environment (light quality and quantity at various times of the day) to generate sympathetically color-matched interior lighting. The possibilities for night lighting with such technology are virtually unlimited, as spaces, walls, floors, and ceilings can be color-washed with light to achieve desired physical, psychological, and emotional effects. In the offices similar uses of light to improve or enhance intellectual abilities and potentials may well be a part of the coming years.

Color is a powerful tool in shaping our world. We have limited its use primarily as a result of our lack of knowledge of how to tap into the power to improve, enrich, and enhance the quality of our lives. And, it is the continuing search for keys to unlocking the power of color that presents one of the most rewarding challenges for young designers today.

Color Marketing Group Glossary of Terms*

1. Color Decision Maker   A color decision maker has the final, authoritative responsibility for the colors that will be marketed. Color decision makers may or may not be color forecasters themselves; indeed, they may receive recommendations from color stylists or color forecasters. However, they are the final arbiters of what colors are marketed.

2. Color Forecaster   A color forecaster is one whose primary job is researching and tracking color trends and who is continuously active in forecasting and selecting colors that will be marketed in two years and beyond. Color forecasters may or may not also be color decision makers. However, they are always doing the work needed to anticipate changes in the worlds of consumer and/or contract color.

3. Color Directions®   The directional change (e.g., warmer/cooler, lighter/darker, clearer/greyer, and/or the relative importance of a hue) a color family may be expected to take in either the consumer or contract marketplace in two years. Color Directions forecasts frequently are variations of existing colors, but sometimes a new color to the market is forecast to be important, trend-defining, or trend-setting and therefore directional.

4. Final Consensus Palette   After the CMG workshop participants have constructed their color boards with input from each workshop member, the Color Directions Steering Committee (workshop captains and co-captains, supervised by the Color Directions Committee Co-Chairs) meets to determine the content of the final palette. They use each workshop's color board and written and verbal comments as input to help them come to a consensus.

   The Color Directions palettes published by CMG represent the consensus-projected color direction. Color Directions palettes are interpreted by CMG members and used as input for determining the colors to be used. They usually are not applied exactly as shown in the consensus palette but are varied to fit market and technical requirements.

*Copyright © 1992 Color Marketing Group. The following terms are printed with permission of the Color Marketing Group.

5. CMG Workshops   With 550 participants, each of the 40 CMG workshops requires prior submission of a completed worksheet to qualify the member for participation at the Spring and/or Fall Conference.

Consumer and Contract Color Directions™
Both of these workshops require participants to be forecasters and/or color decision makers who forecast color directions for products which will be in the marketplace in a time frame of *two or more years* (see previous definitions). In Consumer Color Directions Forecast Workshops, members must work at forecasting and be involved in consumer work at least 35 percent of their time. In Contract Workshops, members must forecast color and be involved in contract work at least 50 percent of their time. Consumer Color Directions Forecast Workshops are held during CMG's Spring Conference; Contract Color Directions Workshops at the Fall Conference.

Colors Current™
The Colors Current palette shows the consensus of colors that are most important in today's markets, in a wide variety of product and graphic applications. These workshops are open to all CMG members who select colors for products which will be in the marketplace in a time frame of *less than two years*, whether they are forecaster, non-forecaster, decision maker, technical, design, marketing, or any other area that involves color. Because these workshops address actual colors in current markets as well as colors CMG members know will appear in the next year, they allow members who take part in any aspect of color work to participate. Colors Current workshops take place at CMG's Spring Conference.

Design Influences
These workshops, open to all CMG members, take place at CMG's Fall Conference. A design background is not necessary to participate, rather an open mind and an awareness of trends is a necessity.

Color Combinations: Consumer and Contract
All CMG members are eligible for these hands-on, creative workshops. The workshops discuss the use of colors as they are marketed when combined with other colors and potentially with other products. The color boards produced reflect the best thinking about the

ways CMG colors may be combined for successful product and graphic representation. Consumer Color Combinations Workshops are held at CMG's Fall Conference; Contract Color Combinations Workshops are held at the Spring Conference.

6. Workshop Captains and Co-Captains   Each CMG Captain and Co-Captain must organize both the verbal and visual input of their workshop participants into both a workshop of color or design board plus provide written notes that give insight as to why the colors or designs were selected.

The Captain takes color chips or designs from the worksheets of individual members and, by grouping them, assembles a basic color or design board for discussion in the workshop sessions.

Through often spirited discussions led by the Captain as facilitator and noted by the Co-Captain, each workshop produces a consensus color or design board and written comments that will be used by the Captain and Co-Captain to represent the workshop's input to the Steering Committee.

7. Hue, Value, and Chroma   Just as a box has three dimensions of height, width, and depth, color has the three dimensions of hue, value, and chroma.

Hue is a color's relative position on the color wheel. It is that attribute of color that tells you if the color is red or green or blue or yellow . . . the color family of a color. Use the words warmer and cooler when describing hue differences.

Value is a color's lightness or reflectivity, as measured against a grey scale from white at the top to black at the bottom. Use the words lighter and darker when describing value differences.

Chroma is a color's intensity, purity, clarity, or saturation, as measured by its departure from greyness. Use the terms clearer and greyer when discussing differences in chroma.

8. Let-down   To allow visualization of the ways CMG's Color Directions Forecast colors may be varied when applied and to make them more immediately useful, CMG frequently publishes "let-downs" of Forecast palettes. While the term let-down specifically refers to a lighter value of a color, for one that is let down in value by adding white, sometimes the chroma will be varied as well. The hue does not change.

9. Metamerism[1]   Metamerism is a scientific description of a common color phenomenon: Two color samples which appear to match under one light source no longer match when viewed under a different light source.

For example, two colors may be a virtually perfect match under daylight, but become a mismatch under incandescent light. This is because the two samples were made using different colorants. The different colorants reflect light differently, giving each sample a different reflectance curve. Whenever two colors appear to match but do not have the same curve, a metameric match exists.

The phenomenon of metamerism can also occur as the light source changes. Just as every color sample has a reflectance curve, every light source has a spectral power distribution curve, which shows the different amounts of energy being emitted at different points in the visible spectrum. A light source is one of three components of a color; the other two are the colored object and the observer (a person or device). Whenever the light source changes, the color must change as well. Metamerism occurs when two matching colors change in different ways, by shifting in different directions.

All light sources and combinations of light sources have different spectral power distribution curves that affect color matches when the reflectance curves of the color samples are different.

10. Geometric Metamerism   Two colored objects may appear as a mismatch even though they are coated with or are made from the same material and are viewed under the same light source. This may be because their surface textures or surface particle sizes or orientations are different. This variation results in geometric metamerism.

---

1. Definition courtesy of ColorCurve® Systems, Inc.

Appendix: International Color Organizations

The following is a list of color organizations, arranged alphabetically by country name.

Grupo Argentino del Color Lic.
R. D. Lozano
INTI División Optica
Cas de Correo 157
1650 San Martín
Buenos Aires
Argentina

Colour Society of Australia
Dr. B. Powell
P.O. Box E 184
St. James
N.S.W. 2000
Australia

Arbeitskreis Farbe der Ove-Olav
Dr. F. Rotter
Fachgruppe Messtechnik
Altgasse 35
A-1163 Wien
Austria

Centre d'Information de la Couleur Belgique
Mme. J. Verschueren van Helden
S.A. Levis N.V.
171 Leuvensesteenweg
B-1800 Vilvoorde
Belgium

Canadian Society for Color
Dr. A. R. Robertson
National Research Council
Division of Physics
Ottawa K1A 0R6
Canada

Chinese Colour Commission
Prof. Shu Yuexin
Shandong Textile Engineering College
Dept. of Colour Science
Qingdao
China

Centre Français de la Couleur
Dr. Robert Sève
15 Passage de la Main d'Or
75011 Paris
France

Deutscher Verband Farbe
Dr. G. Geutler
Institut für Lichttechnik, TU
Einsteinufer 19
D-10587 Berlin
Germany

The Colour Group
Dr. M. R. Pointer
Kodak Ltd., Res. Div.
Headstone Drive
Harrow, Middlesex HA1 4TY
Great Britain

Nederlandse Vereniging voor Kleurenstudie
Dr. C. H. Kleemans
Zuidlaan 22
NL-211 GC Aerdenhout
Holland

Hungarian National Colour Committee
Dr. A. Nemcsisc
Technical University of Budapest
Muegyetem rkp. 3
H-1111 Budapest
Hungary

Colour Group of India
Dr. N. S. Gangakhedkar
Compute Spectra Pvt. Ltd.
1, Manisha, Malviya Road
Vile Parle (E)
Bombay 400 057
India

Associazione Ottica Italiana
Prof. L. R. Ronchi
Instituto Nazionale di Ottica
6 Largo Fermi
I-50125 Firenze
Italy

Color Science Association of Japan
A. Kodama
Japan Color Research Institute
1-19 Nishiazabu 3 Ch
Minato-Qu
Tokyo 106
Japan

Jafca, Japan Fashion Color Association
Mr. Bunta Idei
Nihon Senshoku Kaikan Bldg.
4 Yonbancho Chiyoda-ku
Tokyo 102
Japan

Nippon Color & Design Research Institute, Inc.
Mr. Shigenobu Kobayashi
8-22 Ichigayadaimachi,
Shinjuku-ku,
162 Tokyo
Japan

Norsk Farveforum
U. Willumsen
P.O. Box 1714 Hystad
N-3200 Sandefjord
Norway

Polish Committee for Standardization
Prof. Dr. Sobczak
ul. Elektroralna 2
PL-139 Warszawa
Poland

South African Colour Science Association
A. N. Chalmers
P.O. Box 36319
Menlo Park
Pretoria 0102
South Africa

Svenska Farggruppen
Th. Hord
Swedish Colour Centre Foundation
P.O. Box 14038
S-10440 Stockholm
Sweden

International Association of Color Consultants
Frank Mahnke
11 Quai Capo d'Istria
Geneva 1205
Switzerland

Schweizerische Lichttechnische Gesellschaft
A. O. Wuillemin
Postfach
CH-8034 Zürich
Switzerland

American Association of Textile Chemists and Colorists
William R. Martin
P.O. Box 12215
Research Triangle Park, N.C. 27709
USA

American Information Center for Color and
    Environment
Mrs. Erna Haynes
3621 Alexia Place
San Diego, Calif. 92116
USA

Color Association of the United States
Dolores Ware
343 Lexington Avenue
New York, NY 10016
USA

Color Marketing Group
Ms. Nancy Burns
4001 North Ninth Street
Suite 102
Arlington, Va. 22203
USA

Dry Color Manufacturers Association
J. L. Robinson
206 N. Washington Street
Alexandria, Va. 22320-1839
USA

International Association of Color Consultants
Rudolf Mahnke
730 Pennsylvania Avenue
San Diego, California 92103
USA

Inter-Society Color Council
Mrs. Joy Turner Luke
Studio 231
Box 18, Route 1
Sperryville, Va. 22740
USA

National Paint and Coatings Association, Inc.
Larry L. Thomas
1500 Rhode Island Avenue, N.W.
Washington, D.C. 20005
USA

Bibliography

Albers, Josef. *The Interaction of Color.* New Haven, Conn.: Yale University Press, 1963.

Anderson, Mary. *Color Therapy: The Application of Color for Healing, Diagnosis & Well-Being.* United Kingdom: Aquarian Press, Thorsons SF.

Birren, Faber. *Light, Color and Environment.* Rev. ed. New York: Van Nostrand Reinhold, 1982.

Eckstein, Helen W. *Color in the 21st Century: A Practical Guide for Graphic Designers, Photographers, Printers . . .* New York: Watson-Guptill, 1991.

Eiseman, Leatrice. *Alive with Color.* Reston, Va.: Acropolis Books, 1983.

————, and Lawrence Herbert. *The Pantone Book of Color.* New York: Harry N. Abrams, Inc., 1990.

Favre, Jean-Paul, and André November. *Color and Communication.* Zurich, Switzerland: ABC Verlag, 1979.

Gerritsen, Frans. *Theory and Practice of Color.* New York: Van Nostrand Reinhold, 1975.

Fisk, Josiah. *Color in Fashion.* Massachusetts: Rockport Publishers, Design Sourcebook Services, 1990.

Kobayashi, Shigenobu. *Color Image Scale.* Tokyo: Kodansha, 1991.

Lenclos, Jean-Philippe, and Dominique Lenclos. *The Colors of France: Architecture and Landscape.* Paris: Moniteur, 1982.

Linton, Harold. *Color Consulting: A Survey of International Color Design.* New York: Van Nostrand Reinhold, 1991.

————. *Color Model Environments.* New York: Van Nostrand Reinhold, 1985.

Lowe Bros. Paint Company. *How to Make Your Home Attractive.* Dayton, Ohio: Lowe Bros. Paint Company, 1914.

Moss, Roger W. *Century of Color.* Watkins Glen, N.Y.: American Life Foundation, 1981.

Norman, Richard B. *Electronic Color.* New York: Van Nostrand Reinhold, 1990.

Pantone Textile Color Selector. Moonachie, N.J.: Pantone, Inc., 1988.

Porter, Tom. *Architectural Color: A Design Guide to Using Color on Buildings.* New York: The Whitney Library of Design, 1982.

Rochon, Richard, and Harold Linton. *Color in Architectural Illustration.* New York: Van Nostrand Reinhold, 1989.

Sherwin-Williams Company. *House Painting.* Cleveland: Sherwin-Williams Company, 1884.

Index

DATE DUE

DE 06 '96		
OC 23 '97		
OCT 31 2000		
NOV 28 2001		

Demco, Inc. 38-293